ELVIS PRESLEY BOULEVARD

ELVIS PRESLEY BOULEVARD

FROM SEA TO SHINING SEA, ALMOST

Mark Winegardner

The Atlantic Monthly Press
New York

FIRST EDITION

Library of Congress Cataloging-in-Publication Data

Winegardner, Mark,   1961–
Elvis Presley Boulevard.

1. United States—Description and travel—1981–
2. Winegardner, Mark, 1961–   —Journeys—United
States.
I.   Title.
E169.04.W57   1987   917.3'04927   87–24180
ISBN 0–87113–205–2

Published simultaneously in Canada
Printed in the United States of America

Second Printing

Designed by Laura Hough

For Laura

Acknowledgments

I am indebted to Steven Bauer, who kicked my butt enough to turn a dilettante with vague, ungainly literary stirrings into a writer.

Thanks also to Christine Prickett, Richard Bausch and Gary Fisketjon, who sharpened both the concept and the writing of this book and who showed me how much can be added by subtraction.

Most of all, I would like to thank my parents, who, year after year, gave me the opportunity to look out any of several windows and see America rolling by.

Contents

Mark Winegardner

ELVIS PRESLEY BOULEVARD

ELVIS PRESLEY BOULEVARD

Preface
Now and Then
There's a Fool
Such as I

For the better part of
every summer as I grew up, RV's filled our driveway.
When I was in grade school, they were always travel-
trailers, but one year I spent weeks talking about how
great it would be to eat, sleep and go to the bathroom
without ever slowing below 55. After that, they were
always motorhomes. The brand names changed—a
Smoky, a Norris, a Titan, two Champions and a dozen
Holiday Ramblers—but their place on the left side of
our driveway, across the street from Moore Park in
Bryan, Ohio, waiting for Mom to pack the paper plates
and paperbacks and for Dad to fill the water tank and
tuck the sewer hose into the rear bumper—all that
stayed the same for years and years.

Mom and Dad ran an RV dealership—Winegardner Mobile Homes, Inc.—but they bought it right
before the first Arab oil embargo and, except for an
odd year here and there, the business was always
shaky. Still, for me, for my sister Shari, and maybe
even for my parents, disappointment in the gradual
failure of the business was eclipsed by its best perk:
demonstrators. Every spring we'd each wander

3

through the sales lot, folding out tables and sofa-beds, opening and closing cabinets and closets, sitting in a chair and imagining what it would be like to sit in that very spot if the unit were loaded to the gills with sleeping bags, Frisbees and sweatshirts and parked in a full-hook-up space in a Safari Campground in the Ozarks.

Then we'd get together and argue about which RV to choose as that year's demonstrator, whereupon the newly selected RV would take its place in our driveway for the first of a series of weekend shakedown trips—little jaunts to places like Ohio Caverns, Pokagon State Park, Cincinnati Reds games or Bronner's Christmas Decoration Museum and Gift Shop in Frankenmuth, Michigan. If everything on the RV worked okay and, more important, if there were enough space inside to keep members of my combative family from killing one another, the travel-trailer or motorhome in question was deemed to have passed, and it was out of the driveway and onto the highway for the Big Trip.

We never went to the same place twice, and I grew up feeling superior to the dullards who spent three weeks every August playing and drinking gin in the same Hilton Head condominium. They were vacationers, but we were sightseers, travelers. We were *tourists.*

I took my first American road trip when I was seven months old, a meandering trek through New England. I loved it, or so my parents claimed. After we got home and unpacked the trailer, Mom says I sobbed for hours after Dad towed the empty trailer out of our driveway.

In grade school I took enormous pleasure in correcting my teachers' mistakes in history and geography by telling them I'd *been* to Yorktown, to Gettysburg, to Vicksburg, to Cripple Creek, wherever. By the time I was sixteen, I'd been in each of the continental United States.

Not that the trips were paradise on wheels. In the travel-trailer days, Shari and I would lean over the front seat of our huge brown Electra, dodging Dad's flailing hand, desperate for a wisp of cool air from the middle air-conditioning vent. And to pass any historical marker or scenic overlook was a mortal sin, regardless of its historic or scenic merits. If I told my parents I was too caught up in a biography of Johnny Unitas to bother getting out of the car, Mom would look hurt and Dad would whack me on the back of the head. And of course, at least once each trip, my parents would get into an argument that sent them teetering on the brink of divorce. One time, in a red-white-and-blue Champion motorhome parked on the beach near Corpus Christi, they banished Shari and me outside for the whole day without so much as a wiffleball while they went at it. We were so bored we didn't even hit each other.

But these summers did instill something in me, a kind of eminently American wanderlust, a love of amusement parks big and small, sparkling and grungy; of reading a different city's newspaper every morning; of roadside souvenir stands in Montana that sell authentic buckskin moccasins; of hanging my feet out the car window, tingling with the danger of oncoming oversize loads, until Mom caught me. A love of crossing state lines.

We'd play license plate games, and getting a Delaware in Oregon or a Nevada in South Carolina or a Hawaii anywhere would spread a happy mist of destiny over the rest of the day. Shari never seemed to catch this. She was also seven months old on her first trip, and she bawled all the way to, through and back from Florida. Rarely, on any trip, did she know where we were or where we were going. She'd ask "Are we there yet?" every fifteen minutes with only the most tenuous idea where "there" might be. On one trip to California, Mom tried to inflict a geography lesson.

"Okay, honey, do you remember what state was before Arizona?"

Shari pursed her lips, then her eyes widened. "Mexico!"

We all laughed.

"Close. That's *New* Mexico," Mom corrected. "Do you remember the one before that?"

Shari showed the beginnings of a pout. "Dallas?"

More laughs.

"Now think, punkin'. Dallas what?" Mom asked.

"Texas?"

"That's right!" Mom gushed. "Good! You know what was before that, don't you?"

Shari, buoyed by her small success, started to smile. "Yeah, I know that. That's easy. Indiana!"

Then Mom started from scratch, finally giving up when she asked Shari the name of the state we'd be in next. "Now stop and *think.*"

"Disendyland."

I nearly always knew where we were, because I spent hours studying maps, looking for oddly named towns we'd never go through, looking up populations of cities in our path, studying the "Transcontinental Mileage Chart" and dreaming about the 3,216 miles that lay between Duluth and Anchorage, calculating how many miles we'd already gone, how many we had to go and—as a consequence of all this—feeling a true sense of accomplishment when I'd successfully endured Kansas.

I was fifteen when we took our last Big Trip as a family, a three-week dash to Washington and Oregon, the only two of the continental forty-eight I hadn't yet been in. Though we fought more on that trip than any other, and it was obvious there wasn't room enough anymore for the four of us in a 27-foot motorhome, I can't remember one specific argument. In my heart I know these were three of the best weeks of my life. I've never been back there, but I still smile when I remember Coeur d'Alene and Spokane, the central Washington desert and the Olympic rain forest, Seattle and Victoria, the fir-lined banks of the Columbia River and the rocky coastline drive that is U.S. 101—all those places that, in my mind, are cast in the deepest greens and blues and silvers.

During that trip, three months before my sixteenth birthday, I learned to drive as I nosed the 27-foot-long Holiday Rambler down I-90 through the desert; and, three years before my drinking-age birthday, I drank my first beer in the presence of my parents at a seafood place on Puget Sound.

We hit I-80 at Salt Lake City, taking dead aim for Bryan, Ohio, 1,637 miles down the same road, the first exit on the Ohio Turnpike. When we got there, I pulled the motorhome into the left side of the driveway and frowned; our house looked as strange and decidedly unfamiliar as it always did when we returned.

I realize now that the poor old thing, with its bricks, its white aluminum siding and its thick concrete foundation, never stood a chance against my memories of the road.

1

If I Can Dream

About noon the sun came out and the rain on Interstate 75 south of Cincinnati began to dry. It was cool for May and still wet enough that the worn tires of Bob Wakefield's 1968 Chevy Impala continued to hiss, although the hissing quieted by the moment; I could hear it incrementally, like the protracted fade of a rock 'n' roll song. That morning we'd left Oxford, Ohio, where we'd been going to graduate school, headed south on the first leg of a two-month transcontinental trip that was my idea all along.

"Do you hear that?" Bob said. "Do you hear that rattle? That must be the timing. It's good that we're not too far away yet."

"I don't hear anything," I said. "Cars like this were engineered for open-road cruising." But a part of me knew he'd welcome the excuse to go home.

"I heard it again." Bob frowned and adjusted his glasses, which—although he's legally blind in one eye—he'd considered a luxury until just last month, when he'd come into a modest inheritance that had bankrolled both the spectacles and this trip.

"You're losing your mind," I said, "or at least your hearing." The only rattle I heard was a subdued rasp that I'd heard every time I'd been in his car. But Bob loved this Impala, much as you might love a loutish, bad-smelling and traitorous childhood friend just because he'd accompanied you through the rites of passage. A midsize car when manufactured, larger than newer vans or pickups, the Impala probably never turned a head, male or female, despite its tentative curves and silly toylike taillights: failed attempts to make the mammoth sedan look contemporary. The body was dented and rusted through, with a finish that hadn't survived Peace with Honor and a paint job now weathered to a shade dimly evocative of blue. I'd convinced Bob to take his car because mine had no radio and wasn't big enough to sleep in—each pretty essential for a two-month trip on a $500 budget. I couldn't spare any more than that, not with an August honeymoon to pay for, along with the consequent real-world debts to come. "All that's happening is that you're burning off the carbon," I said. I didn't know what this meant, but I'd once heard a mechanic use the phrase.

"It's the timing," Bob said, "or maybe one of the valves. Do you know how much a valve job costs?"

"No." I felt thirteen again, when a senior forced me to guess how much a sixpack cost and I said $10. "You tell me."

"More than El Basurero's worth. Minimum of five hundred."

El Basurero, a lovely name for an unlovely thing. Having decided that the vehicle of any quest must have a name, Bob settled for this, which he claimed was Spanish for either "the garbage heap" or "the garbage man."

"Look!" I shouted. "Our first Stuckey's sign!"

In no other country on this
planet can you travel so far on good roads without
crossing a national border or getting roughed up by
the secret police, and this alone makes American mo-
toring mythic and unique.

Abetting this process are the roads themselves,
the United States Interstate Highway System. Though
it is much maligned, you'd have to go some to find an
American institution that makes more sense, that im-
poses more order on chaos. Solely from the number
of an interstate highway, you can tell where you are.
Even numbers are east-west routes, with numbering
beginning in the deep south and increasing as it moves
north; odd numbers are north-south roads, with numbering beginning in the far west and increasing as it
moves east. Therefore you can know, without needing
to be told, that I-10 connects Jacksonville with Los
Angeles; I-90, Providence with Seattle; I-5, San Diego
with Vancouver; I-95, Miami with New York. Three-
digit routes have their own code: if the first digit is
even, the road circles a city; if odd, the road is a spur
into the city.

Some might argue that this system was in-
stituted less to impose order than to allow interstates
to be told apart, because, after all, they all look alike.
But my mother taught me to distrust people who use
the phrase "they all look alike."

Skirting the interstates at predictable intervals
are a series of what snobs call tourist traps. There are
three ways of looking at these. First, you can dismiss
them as a glut of awful polyester, a synthetic attraction interesting only to hayseeds, simpletons and stupendous dunderheads. Second, you can consider
them legitimate attractions, if you're either unable or
unwilling to distinguish between the craftsmanship
that produced the Hollywood Wax Museum and that
which produced the Rocky Mountains. Third, you can

take it all at its own level, seeing a tourist trap as a tourist trap, enjoying a pink flamingo, an Elvis Presley ashtray or the Cadillac Ranch—a row of vintage Caddies planted nose-down, fins-up—for what they are: amusing windows on the world we inhabit.

I like to pretend I do the third, but I'm guilty of all three.

Which is why I find so many American travel books pompous and sentimental: they focus on out-of-the-way hamlets and undertake microcosmic studies of "our country," thereby making us long for the past. That's valid, I suppose, but I'm more interested in the macrocosm. I don't doubt that Nameless, Tennessee, can be a splendid place to visit. But if everyone goes to Gatlinburg, Graceland and Disneyland, to Ruby Falls, the Sears Tower and the French Quarter, then it's irrational to dismiss out of hand what can be learned in such tourist meccas. And while I like traveling the back roads as well as the next person, the road we all share—our common road—is the turnpike, with its tollbooths and off-ramps, its service plazas and truckstops, its residents and its transients.

Somewhere in central Kentucky, near Big Bone Lick State Park, we stopped at a Stuckey's for gasoline, batteries for my tape recorder and a pecan log. "Don't buy any of the other candy," Bob warned, pointing at the faded, dusty boxes. "That's been here since the war—and I don't mean Vietnam, which was a police action."

"We're on vacation," I told the cashier. "We're tourists."

"Yeah, well, I get a lot of tourists in this store," she said, taking my money. "Where you bound?"

"Gatlinburg. But that's just for tonight. Then we're going to zig-zag all over America. Anyplace special you think we ought to go?"

She shrugged. "I've never left Kentucky."

"Seriously?"

The woman glanced toward the turtle clusters, averting my eyes, as if I'd evoked a specific memory. "I went to Cincinnati once. And to Chicago, but I was too young to remember."

I couldn't fathom why she never hopped in a car and drove in random fashion until the world looked substantially different from central Kentucky. But rather than ask her, I pocketed my change.

"Son!" she called as I was leaving and a bell clacked against the glass of the door. "Where all are you going in that thing?"

I couldn't help myself; I heard our itinerary coming out of my mouth: "Florida, New Orleans, Memphis, Chicago, Colorado, Arizona, Las Vegas, Los Angeles, San Francisco. Then back to Ohio, where we come from."

"Don't drink and drive," she said.

Back in the car Bob calculated the gas mileage, writing the figures in a red leatherette account book. The first entry on the first page read: "Account book, $3.18." He looked more pleased than when I'd gone in to pay. "Over seventeen miles per gallon," he said. "I haven't gotten over seventeen since high school."

I got behind the wheel and attempted to wrestle El Basurero back onto I-75.

"No. No, no, no." Bob waved his hands in disgust. "That's neutral."

"*What's* neutral? It says P right there."

"It doesn't work anymore. Can't you feel when it's in drive?"

"I looked at the thing and it said D, so I hit the gas. How was I supposed to know?"

"Okay. Now you know." He put the account book back in the glove compartment. "Now you're supposed to know."

Bob Wakefield and I both grew up in small Ohio towns, and we both were in the same freshman English class at Miami University. We met near the end of the term, when we were assigned to the same workshop group, along with three others, to revise an essay about roller coasters. Bob and I were worse than worthless, as we got caught up in a discussion of Disneyland's swirling, spinning teacups and how they were actually scarier than any roller coaster.

Thereafter we were friends, though for the next several years "friendly acquaintances" would've been more accurate. We were writers of some local renown: I was a hack columnist on the student newspaper, and Bob was the darling of undergraduate poetry workshops and the editor of *Dimensions*, a campus literary magazine.

During finals week, second semester, senior year, I ran into Bob in the *Dimensions* office, hunched over a shabby wooden desk, reading *The Brothers Karamazov.* We were both in trouble. Bob had to read five Russian novels and write a paper; I had to write what was supposed to be a semester-long journal for a fiction class. We studied together for a while, happy to find someone else so impossibly robbed of sleep. He zipped through Dostoevsky as other people do Jackie Collins, and when I charged that he couldn't possibly be absorbing much at that rate, he lit into an animated synopsis that could have gotten him a job with the Cliff's Notes people. I stayed long enough to finish

13

February and for Bob to come up with a paper title: "Serf's Up."

That fall, because of a complicated series of events, most of which had everything to do with laziness, we found ourselves back at Miami, going after master's degrees in creative writing. This had been our safety net, an if-all-else-fails option, and all else had failed.

Bob and I became close friends that year. He didn't have a radio or a television or even any furniture, so he spent a lot of time on my sofa. We swapped hometown stories (which have since run together in my mind) and played several hundred Trivial Pursuit matches, against all levels of competition, all but one of which Bob won. This game might not be the most reliable barometer of intelligence, but it's a good example of the kind of formidable, encyclopedic knowledge Bob had amassed. Sometimes I got the feeling that he hadn't learned any more than I had, but where I forgot all the chemistry and geography I crammed for and parroted back on exams, Avogodro's Number and the elevation of Lake Titicaca have stuck to Bob like flies to flypaper. He really can read Russian novels in one sitting, too, and then write the best paper in the class.

In the spring I pitched the trip to Bob as an affordable alternative to the clichéd, pretentious, summer-long pan-European treks of the rich and unimaginative. He agreed to take at least the first leg with me, after which he might get a job waiting tables at a restaurant his sister managed in Estes Park, Colorado. Eager for a companion who had a car to volunteer, I took Bob's response as an unequivocal "yes."

After making a list of all our friends and relatives who lived in interesting places, we subdivided it into a "C list" (people who would let us sleep on their floor), a "B list" (people who would let us sleep in a bed) and an "A list" (people who would not only let us sleep in a bed but also feed us).

When I told Laura about the trip, she accepted it, even though she'd have to handle the bulk of the wedding plans alone. Her only spoken misgiving was that she questioned my motives. I told her I didn't even *know* my motives, and that I was going in order to discover them.

On Thursday, May 31, 1984—with Laura's WATS-line at work scribbled on the back of a leftover Winegardner Mobile Homes business card in my wallet—Bob Wakefield and I packed up his Impala and hit the high road.

We finished the Stuckey's pecan log near Daniel Boone National Forest. "We have anything else to eat," Bob asked.

"I don't know," I said, still uncomfortable with the boxy, drifting feel of El Basurero. At least the road was dry now. "Go ahead and look." Right before we left I'd thrown the contents of my refrigerator and cabinets into a Playmate cooler, but I'd already forgotten what all there was.

Bob sifted through the cooler and found snack cakes, peanut butter, soggy bread and beer.

I laughed. "The five basic food groups of travel."

"You forgot circus peanuts." Bob is a devotee of circus peanuts, goober-shaped marshmallow candies manufactured in my hometown. He likes to eat them and marvel that they're considered food. "I still can't believe the mileage we got."

"It's a sign," I said. "But I don't know of what."

We had all the windows rolled down, and the wind slapped us silly.

The summer after I graduated, I couldn't find a job for over a month and wound up as a part-time lifeguard and bartender at Bryan's only country club. I spent the summer in a postadolescent, self-pitying funk, resenting how unfair it was that these superficial dentists made more money than I probably ever would. I drank too much and maintained the pose of a writer, though I didn't write a word.

One night I was playing cards with the few hometown friends I still had when one of them suggested we take a few beers, go lie on one of the greens at the club's golf course and look at the stars. This, I thought, was a stupid idea. But since I couldn't bear to play the summer's seven hundredth hand of seven-card stud, I went along.

There were about a dozen of us. Two other guys worked for the club, but I was the only one there who was not a member. We spread our blankets and sat down on the tenth green. Abruptly I decided I'd had it.

"I'm making a pilgrimage to Elvis's grave. Who wants to go with me?"

Everyone laughed.

"If we leave now," I said, "we'll be there by morning."

But I couldn't solicit a sidekick.

I had no idea what had brought on this impulse, but suddenly Elvis Presley and Graceland and everything he and it represented—though I had no concrete idea what that might be—were the most magical things in the world. If I hadn't been afraid I'd fall asleep, I'd have driven there alone.

As it was, I nearly did anyway. At about one in the morning, I got in my car to go home, a three-mile drive. Halfway there, I spun the wheel sharply and, spitting pea gravel into the ditch, headed south down Ohio 576. Here I go, I thought, to Memphis. Going to see the King.

I had no map, but I figured I could drive south until dawn, then stop at a convenience store and write down all the directions from a Rand McNally map on their magazine rack. No money, either, but I had credit cards. I could call my parents from, say, Louisville, so they won't call the cops.

I pulled onto the grassy shoulder of the road right before the intersection of 576 and U.S. 6 near the Defiance County line. Turning off the ignition, I leaned my head on the steering wheel and closed my eyes to think. At sunrise I woke up and drove home.

Near the Kentucky-Tennessee line, we first noticed the billboards. And a good 25 miles before we got to Gatlinburg, Tennessee, the billboards took over. VISIT GATLINBURG'S WAX MUSEUM, one red-white-and-blue sign said, and a little square within it invited America's tourists to "See ELVIS!!" Then came one for Silver Dollar City, featuring a grizzled prospector panning for gold in a rock-choked stream and staking a claim to "The Best Variety of Family Attractions." And so it went, with boards for Porpoise Island, the House of Illusions, Stars Over Gatlinburg Wax Museum, Ripley's Believe It or Not Museum, Guinness Book of World Records

Museum and the Smoky Mountain Auto Museum, which employed 10-foot-tall letters to boast about its possession of Sheriff Buford T. Pusser's Death Car.

"If Lady Bird Johnson goes to hell," Bob said, "I'll bet they make her spend every day driving down a replica of this road."

Giant water slides and elaborate miniature golf courses lined the highway as we entered Pigeon Forge, Gatlinburg's northern suburb. On the right, beside a package liquor store and a Spur gas station, was a green, two-story motor lodge. When I saw the sign for the place, I had no choice but to pull El Basurero into the parking lot.

ELVIS MUSEUM, read the top part of the huge sign, a royal blue crown dotting the *i* of *Elvis*. And in smaller letters underneath: "world's largest . . . COLLECTION"; a collection of what, it did not say. But underneath that was the name of the place, and the reason I'd stopped. The Elvis Presley Heartbreak Motel.

There had been no billboards dispensing advance word of this.

The Heartbreak Motel was U-shaped and vaguely Alpine in its architecture, with a bush-filled courtyard in the middle and the Elvis Museum at the base of the U. Out front a wooden facsimile of a street sign read ELVIS PRESLEY BLVD., referring, as near as I could figure, to the parking lot. A 1955 yellow-and-black Cadillac was parked beside the street sign, so I gripped its fins and posed for a picture.

Just inside the door to the museum was a giftshop full of Elvis souvenirs and a tired-looking woman behind a counter that served as motel registration desk, giftshop cash register and museum ticket booth. The "museum" was the room directly behind her.

Bob picked up a foot-long cylinder of hard

candy that spelled, of course, "Elvis." There was a sticker on the cellophane that covered the candy, and Bob read it aloud. " 'Elvis's name goes all the way through the candy.' " He laughed. "Wonder if it really does."

"It really does," the woman said, nodding. "The other day we ate a piece just to see." A garish painting of Elvis grinned at us over her right shoulder, a dull gold chain taped to his neck. I doubt I'd have known it was Elvis had we not been at the Heartbreak Motel.

We walked around, doing what tourists are supposed to do in giftshops: picking things up, showing them to each another, trying on silly hats, moving all the moving parts of elaborate gee-gaws, all with no intention of spending any money. This is free entertainment, and only the most insufferable highbrow could deny the pleasure to be had in running one's hands through a box of rubber jumping frogs with Elvis tattoos on their bellies.

From what we could see in the giftshop and through a gap in the curtain to the back room, we decided the museum wasn't worth the $4 admission. Most of the memorabilia had belonged not to Elvis but to J. D. Sumner, the guitar player during Presley's Vegas years. There looked to be a lot of pictures of J.D. and Elvis together, J.D. in cowboy shirts and bolo ties, Elvis in tinted glasses and capes of incessant rhinestones.

On our way out Bob turned, walked up to the desk and, pointing past the woman, asked, "I'm curious. Is that a commissioned portrait of Elvis over there, or is it just someone who admired him?"

I couldn't tell if she noticed Bob's patronizing tone.

"I'm not really sure," she said. "It's not the orig'-nal oll, and we kept saying, 'That can't be Elvis Presley, it doesn't look like Elvis Presley.' But we found out it's been done from an actual photograph."

"An actual photograph, huh?" Bob said. "It looks a little like Robert Goulet."

The woman smiled. "The orig'nal oll of this painting is hanging on the wall in Graceland Mansion."

"Oh, we're going there," I said brightly. "But we're going to Florida first."

The woman smiled, but it was clear she thought we were hopelessly insane. In her book the road to Memphis took you through Nashville. In ours it meandered through marshes and bayous, then upstream against the Mississippi.

2

Are You Lonesome Tonight?

My family visited Gatlinburg in 1972 to prove to my sister the existence of bears and Indians.

Shari suffered the normal disillusions of childhood more acutely than most kids. First she learned there was no such thing as the Easter Bunny. Then she caught Dad trying to slip a quarter under her pillow, and the Tooth Fairy's gig was up. But when a kid in her kindergarten class (there is always one such kid; I'm sure you've met him) told her Santa Claus was an elaborate parental hoax, Shari returned home announcing that she'd quit believing not only in Santa Claus but also in bears and Indians.

Mom confessed that Santa Claus was made up, but insisted that bears and Indians were real. During a National Geographic special, Mom called Shari downstairs to see the bears.

"TV is all pretend," Shari said. "There's no such thing as Gilligan. There's no such thing as Sonny and Cher." Crying, she ran upstairs.

That summer we went to the Smoky Mountains, in search of bona fide bears and Indians.

Just inside Great Smoky Mountain National Park, Shari saw her first bear, mooching Wonder Bread from foolhardy tourists (not us, for a change). Her jaw dropped open, and when she regained a little composure, she began singing "I believe in bears" incessantly, to no particular tune at all, until I broke down and slugged her one, and Dad spanked me with his old fraternity paddle. All in all, your basic family tourism.

But to see a real Indian we had to drive all the way through the park, towing a 29-foot travel-trailer, to Cherokee, North Carolina. "We're going to an Indian reservation, kids," Mom said, and, reading from a brochure, she told us about the migratory problems of the Cherokee tribe. Shari pressed her nose to the window, straining to see her first Indian.

"Look!" Mom whispered as we stopped at the first traffic light in Cherokee.

An elderly Indian woman, dressed in beaded buckskin and wearing moccasins, waited to cross the street. All four of us gawked shamelessly. I couldn't believe how *authentic* the woman looked, and I wondered if she wore this clothing all the time. The woman also stared, past us to our trailer, her eyes sweeping across its laminated shell.

"Mommy, is that—" Shari started to ask.

"Shhh!" Mom said. "Yes."

We watched as the woman continued sizing up our implausibly long rig, until her eyes met ours. She jumped a little, and we must have, too. But before we could demurely look away, the woman broke into a broad grin.

My family rolled on through Cherokee, groggy from cross-cultural pollination. "I believe in bears and Indians," Shari sang. "And ghosts and tigers and witches and frogs and Santa Claus."

I' drove El Basurero down the main drag of Gatlinburg just as the shadows started to lengthen. Nearly everything on both sides of the street had been flashed on at least twenty billboards along U.S. 441. We decided we had enough money to see one and only one tourist attraction, so I parked the car on a side street and we set about choosing a sight to see.

The first candidate: Xanadu, a Foam House of Tomorrow. I don't pretend to know what Coleridge, Kubla Khan or even Olivia Newton-John would've thought about this, but to me it looked like a shaving-cream sculpture of Flintstone dwellings. A sign in front explained how this mighty pleasure dome was filled with post-modern furniture, German kitchen appliances and Swedish stereo equipment. The brochure I'd picked up cryptically promised us we'd "Marvel at a first-of-a-kind Champagne Glass Bed and Children's Swiss Cheese Playroom."

"Want to go in here?"

Bob shook his head. "There'll be better things than this. Anyway, that could never be the house of tomorrow, not really. It'd make people feel like bees."

The Stars Over Gatlinburg Wax Museum was ruled out when we decided the pictures of Robin Williams and Marilyn Monroe in their brochure looked more like Lawrence Welk and Elizabeth Montgomery. We passed on the Ripley's museum, too, when—after Bob figured out the secret behind the lobby display, a faucet suspended in the air that appeared to gush water—the ticket lady sniffed and said, "You think you're smart? I got me a four-year-old grandson, took him thirty seconds to figure that out." Believe it.

The House of Illusions looked a little tackier than most. Out front stood a mannequin of Carrie Fisher in her Princess Leia *Star Wars* garb, but I doubt I'd have known that without the white robe, the cinnamon-roll hairdo, the aluminum R2-D2 whirring and beeping beside her, and a little placard at her feet that read "Princess Leia."

"Hi there," a woman's voice said.

Bob and I looked around. We were alone on the threshold of the House of Illusions.

"I'm in here," the voice said. "In the window, there to your right, in the bottle."

Behind that window was a mannequin Arab, a couple handfuls of costume jewelry, thousands of fake gold coins, sand and—right in the middle—a glass bottle with a flickering image of a genie inside.

"My name's Jeannie," the genie said. She was sitting cross-legged on satin pillows, smoking a cigarette. She wasn't making direct eye contact, so I figured she was in a room in the back and they were using mirrors to reflect her image into the bottle. "I'm going on vacation pretty soon."

"Where you going," I asked, wondering why she wasn't trying to entice us into the House of Illusions. Isn't she on commission?

"I'm going to Carolina Beach."

"After you get out of the bottle, right?" I said.

"Yeah. I'm sorta travelin' to all the beaches. Myrtle Beach, Carolina Beach." She stubbed out her cigarette in an ashtray balanced on her lap, then busied herself with the lighting of a new one. She looked to be a good forty pounds overweight, though weight's hard to gauge on someone smaller than a Barbie doll. "Good place for a nice suntan, huh?"

"I guess," Bob said.

"I had one, but it sorta faded away."

"It's hard to get a tan in a bottle," I said.

"Yeah, tell me about it."

Bob pointed at the mannequin Arab. "Who's this big guy with the pointy ears here?"

"Oh, that's my bodyguard. Don't worry about him. Hey, do you guys like to drink? You want me to tell you a real good place to go?" And then, smiling, she added, "As long as you take me with you. You can get me out of this bottle or I'll fly up there on my magic carpet. I can't guarantee us comin' back down—I might run into the mountain—but at least we can get up there."

"Maybe we could take the magic ski lift," Bob said, "or drive our magic car." He shifted his weight from one foot to the other. "Um, don't you get a lot of smoke congested in there?"

"Nope. See, these are Genie 100's. The smoke evaporates. They just stunt your growth."

"They seem to have been very effective," Bob said.

"Yeah, tell me about it. I'm only five inches tall. I grow up just a little bit when I'm out of here, though. Why don't you two let me out? Just go through the glass there and pull the top off."

"That's impossible," I said.

"Nothing's impossible."

"It's impossible for *me*. I've never gone through glass without breaking it. Actually, I've never gone through glass and broken it. I've just never gone through glass."

"It does sorta hurt if it breaks, huh? I sorta got cut this morning."

"Going through glass?" I asked.

"No. Pickin' up motor parts."

"You're the first genie I ever met who picks up motor parts."

"They got one in Myrtle Beach." Then Jeannie sat up straight and let out a long stream of smoke. "Hey, poor Artie 2 just broke down." We turned around, and, sure enough, R2-D2 was neither whirring nor beeping.

Bob took advantage of the opening. "Well, I think we're going to take a stroll up and down the street before it gets dark. What's on up there?"

Jeannie paused to reach in her pack of Salems for another Genie 100. She lit it and took the first long drag.

"Lots of things, huh?" I said, waiting.

Jeannie shrugged. "Really nothin'. They got the World of the Unexplained down there. They got some arcades down there. I like arcades."

As we started to walk away, I still expected her to give us a pitch for the House of Illusions, but all she said was, "Maybe I'll see you up there. On the mountain, I mean." Sure, we said, inching away and breaking free. Behind us a teenager carrying a metal screwdriver tray ambled out of the House and started to remove poor Artie 2's breastplate. Behind him a sign promised a spectacular laser illusion that would allow us to see Elvis sing again. We kept going.

Gatlinburg is perched on the northern edge of Great Smoky Mountain National Park, and, consequently, in the heart of Appalachia. But the steady ebb and flow of tourists keeps the locals from sliding too far toward the pickups-on-blocks-in-the-frontyard stereotype. If you walk two blocks off the main strip of motels and tourist attractions, to the employee parking lots, you'll see scores of spanking-new Broncos and Trans Ams, Tennessee plates firmly bolted on.

Gatlinburg is also a National Park fringe town. There's one of these next to every heavily visited National Park, and their function, so far as I can tell, is to present a gaudy spectacle of dog-eared artifice, leaving visitors flatfooted for the park's suckerpunch of natural splendor. On your way out, the fringe town thrusts you into a world antithetical to the park's emerald mountainsides and silver-flecked waterfalls, an abrupt, unsubtle but necessary transition that enforces your return to the workaday world of studied paper-shuffling and at-the-limit charge accounts. Since Great Smoky Mountain National Park is the most visited of all parks—even Yellowstone, Yosemite and the Grand Canyon—Gatlinburg has become the epitome of the fringe-towns, an amalgam of high-gloss sideshows and custom-made-sweatsock shops.

Geographically, Gatlinburg is both in the South and the Mideast but belongs, really, to neither. It's as close to the Mississippi as it is to the Atlantic, as close to Birmingham, Alabama, as it is to Oxford, Ohio. Confederate flags fly in the rear windows of many a pickup, and country-and-western twangs on many a car radio. Yet the stacks of Yankee and Rebel hats in the souvenir stores are the same height, and the proprietors will happily sew your name on either.

Finally, and certainly most strangely, Gatlinburg is stuffed in a crack in time between the America of the 1940s, which gave us the wonderful corridor of neon that was Route 66, and the America of the 1980s, which gave us the glossy high-tech science fair of the Epcot Center. There's no mistaking the former in the forest-green lodges on the banks of the Little Pigeon River or in the stuffed blackbears set out in front of giftshops to pose for Polaroids. But Gatlinburg's boom years have long passed, and some of those old attractions haven't aged well. Attempts at the latter, the newer frontiers of American tourism like Xanadu, A Foam House of Tomorrow, seem unspeakably awkward. Walt Disney knew how to combine tensile steel, rough-hewn logs, sculptured shrubbery and brightly painted concrete into a timeless ball of magic. Gatlinburg invested everything in pink stucco and aquamarine aluminum, and that has made all the difference.

In a town where The World of the Unexplained can be called "really nothin'" by a chain-smoking, motor-part toting Tennessee genie, anything you choose to do stands to be about equal to anything else you could do. Though we spent well over an hour trying to select our attraction, we finally walked into the Gatlinburg Wax Museum on a whim, after I told Bob about a wax museum I'd seen on a long-ago family vacation that had a Chamber of Horrors section, complete with gallows and guillotines, electric chairs and torture racks, fiends ranging from Vlad the Impaler to Jack the Ripper and Charles Manson, plus vats and vats of shiny wax blood.

But in the Gatlinburg Wax Museum's Blackbeard the Pirate display, any terror the three butchered crewmen might have engendered was overwhelmed by the doily Blackbeard wore at his throat and the grandmotherly figure who seemed to be sniffing the left hand of a henchman. A humming electric motor rolled the whole scene like a comfortable rocking chair.

Nearby, during the signing of the Declaration of Independence, John Adams looked like Yoda, Benjamin Franklin like he'd been surprised by a sudden, heroic erection digging into his right thigh. A hall of recent American presidents portrayed Nixon as a bloated, hairless mole, Carter as one of those apple-head folk dolls, and Reagan as an extra from one of the *Planet of the Apes* movies, which for all I know he was. A diorama of the Battle of the Alamo included, incredibly enough, not even one bucket of wax blood.

The roadside signs for the Gatlinburg Wax Museum had exhorted us to "SEE ELVIS!!" and, in this respect at least, the place did not disappoint. We stood face-to-face with a wax, vaguely Oriental-looking Elvis, sporting Las Vegas clothes on a Louisiana-Hayride body. Bob pushed the button, and—with "Love Me Tender" wafting around us, as soft and mournful as a train in the next county—a Midwestern voice came on to tell us The Legend of the King, sanitary enough for any public-school textbook.

The poorly paced biography dove blandly from comic specificity—Elvis's first guitar, purchased in 1949, cost $12.95—to staggering oversimplification, covering the period from his discharge from the army to his death in two curt sentences. It traced the formative years most carefully: Elvis's stillborn twin Jesse, Elvis's youth in a two-room Tupelo shack, his chronic shyness, his abrupt transition from $35-a-week truckdriver to global sex god.

"He planned to leave on a twelve-day personal appearance tour in August," the voice concluded. "But it wasn't meant to be. On August 16th, 1977, Elvis died. The man is gone. But the legend will live forever."

It bugged me that the story set up all the fairytale elements, then bailed out when our hero didn't live happily ever after. Fairy tales are tough enough to extrapolate from real life without the horrible burden of an untidy ending: the King of Rock 'n' Roll died of a drug overdose, bloated and naked and alone on his bathroom floor.

Bob and I stopped in the museum's giftshop for the trip's first batch of five-for-a-buck postcards. The old man behind the cash register stared out a window, ignoring us as we stood there, the only other people in the shop, waiting to pay for our cards. Bob cleared his throat, the man turned, took the cards and rang them up. "Where'll you be mailing these, boys?"

"Excuse me?" I said.

"Don't mean to be nosy," the man said. "It's just that I'm a retired postman, or what you now call your letter carrier. Never liked that name, 'letter carrier.' Made it sound like we couldn't carry packages, too."

"These will be going all over America," Bob said. "But mostly to Ohio, I guess."

The cash register churned, and Bob and I dug out $1.06 in change. "There's a lot of mail goes out of here to Ohio," the man said. "Folks from Ohio seem to leave the state pretty often . . . no offense."

"None taken," I said. "So, what brought you to this place?"

He slipped the cards into a thin brown bag and handed them to Bob, who pulled out his favorite—a depiction of Nathan Hale on the brink of immortality—and studied it, shaking his head in bemusement.

"My wife's the manager here," the man said. "This ain't too bad, really. It gets me out of the house. Right at the present, we're not having too much business, but it'll begin to pick up now, first of June."

"I have a question," Bob asked. "Are all your wax-figures made here in town?"

"Oh no," the man said. "These aren't done here. These are done in California. Some from Spain. Some from Taiwan, the ones of the stars."

I looked back at him as we left, but he was already staring out the window. He'd love to deliver those postcards, I thought, but he couldn't have given a damn to have sold them.

$\mathbf{A}$ big problem with visiting tourist meccas on our budget, we learned, was that five bucks a day doesn't buy a whole lot of food. In

Gatlinburg you're lucky to find a burger and fries for that. Right then, we easily could have afforded an $8.50 all-you-can-eat smorgasbord, but we were in this for the long haul and, fearful of setting a bad precedent, we stopped instead at a carryout for jelly, yogurt, sodas, a loaf of white bread and a small box of plastic cutlery. Then we repaired to El Basurero, treating ourselves to crumbly peanut-butter-and-jelly sandwiches on the tattered, mildewed front seat of a seventeen-and-a-half-year-old Chevrolet.

As Bob sat on the driver's side and began assembling the sandwiches, I looked for a little dinner music on the car radio. Nothing on FM except polka music and Barbara Mandrell, but on AM I hit familiar territory.

"Reds game!" Bob said, brightening.

Sure enough, though we were nearly 300 miles southeast of Cincinnati, this was WLW, "the 50,000 watt clear-channel voice of the Cincinnati Reds," the same station I'd listened to on summer nights as a boy—200 miles due north of Riverfront Stadium—lying in my bed, the room lit only by the radio dial as I tried to keep awake until the Reds finished off the Dodgers, 2,225 miles to the west.

Darkness had settled over Gatlinburg. Jim and I ate in relative silence, each pleased to have found this tie to his youth in such unlikely surroundings. WLW faded in and out, and I had to fiddle with the knob every thirty seconds. But we could hear it, we were happy, and we were as unprepared as we possibly could have been for the piercing white strobe and swirling red cherrytop of the police car that swooped in from nowhere and pulled up behind us.

The cop got out of his cruiser and walked tightly against the driver's side of El Basurero, as if he expected us to be armed and dangerous. "Lemme see your driver's license," he said, and Bob fished his out.

The cop stuck his head in the window; he was no older than us and, except for a touch of icy wariness in his eyes, looked nothing like a cop. "Yours, too," he said to me. I handed over my driver's license and wondered, for a moment, if Gatlinburg had some sort of law prohibiting the eating of sandwiches in parked cars.

"Uh, could you tell me what the problem is?" Bob said.

The cop studied our licenses, looking from Bob's to mine, back to Bob's again, back to mine, then comparing our photos to our faces, first Bob, then me, then Bob, then me. Finally he handed them back. "I drove by here three times in the last ten minutes, and every one of those three times, you there Mister, uh, Wongunner, you was bendin' over out of sight."

Oh, no, I thought. "I was adjusting the radio," I said. "We're trying to get a baseball game, and it kept fading out." Baseball, get it? We're *guys,* officer.

"Uh-huh," the cop said. Another cruiser, going the other way, slowed as it passed, and our cop waved. I've got these faggots under control, the wave said. "You two stay put," he told us, walking back to the cruiser.

Bob and I turned to watch him. He reached in, said something into his mike and walked back to the driver's-side door. "What brings you two to Gatlinburg?"

"We're on vacation," Bob said. "We stopped here for a snack."

"Well, you know you can't sleep here. On the street, I mean. In your car. We got plenty of motels."

"We're driving on to Chattanooga tonight," I said.

The cop nodded. "Well, you take care then." And he was gone.

Bob and I ranted at each other. The *nerve* of

that guy. What did he think we were up to? Did people arrive daily to sleep on the streets of Gatlinburg? While we finished eating and ranting, police cruisers slid by in both directions, one every few minutes. It was hard to admit, and harder to know how he'd known, but the cop had our number. We *had* planned to sleep there.

W e decided to drive up the mountain, to the only bar we'd ever had recommended to us by a genie. The plan was to meet some women, tell them of our adventure and hope they'd at least invite us to spend the night on their couch. Failing that, the bar would probably stay open until two, maybe three, and if the music was loud enough to keep us awake, we figured we could chew up half the night.

We should have taken the magic tramway. The road up the mountain was far too steep and tortuous for El Basurero *de los muchos años.* Bob bit his lip and wrestled the wheel from left to right to left to right—never was there 30 yards of straight road. I switched off the radio and sat in the nervous silence adopted only by defendants waiting for juries to return verdicts and by passengers in cars that might at any moment fly off the road. I imagined all the mystical parts with functions far beyond my ken—the differential and the U-joint, the timing system and the drive train—and how they might snap, drop off or explode.

But the Chevy made it, sputtering and growling, right into the newly blacktopped parking lot of the monstrous chalet that was Ober Gatlinburg.

I knew Ober Gatlinburg was a ski lodge in sea-

33

son, a restaurant and scenic overlook during the day, but I didn't know what to expect on a cold night on the eve of June. In the daytime an aerial tramway the size of a garage crept up and down a thick steel cable, filled with camera-toters. I remember taking that ride with my family a dozen years before, and being struck by the view from the top: the chrome and blacktop of Gatlinburg in one direction, the relentless green of Great Smoky Mountain National Park in the other. But at night the tramway shuts down, the tourists return to their motor courts and even the view disappears. All I could see of Gatlinburg was scattered streetlights, and the park was invisible under the cover of night.

The main door opened onto a ballroom, and an oom-pah-pah band oomped its last few pah-pahs to six drunken patrons. All but two tables had been cleared, and an employee in lederhosen fidgeted by the cash register, glowering at the remaining revelers. "Is there a bar around here?" I asked him.

"A bar?"

"You know, a bar. This, um, woman told us there's sort of like a hangout up here."

"Oh, you mean the *dis-* co. Go through that door. It's on the left. You can't miss it."

The place was decorated in the manner of all American nightclubs in the six months following the release of *Saturday Night Fever:* two mirror balls and a network of strobing neon on the ceiling, upholstered conversation pits along the walls, each with little two-foot-tall wooden cubes in the middle, painted to look like dice and intended as a place for dancers to set half-drunk Seven-and-Sevens. Two young women—a blonde and a brunette—danced with each other, while two bearded men and a stringy-haired woman occupied the conversation pit along the far wall. Over Michael Jackson's "Billie Jean," Bob and I shouted for two drafts.

"Billie Jean" finished and a Van Halen song started up. The dancers sat down a few barstools away from us. They were dressed in MTV-chic—miniskirts, ceramic earrings, purple eye makeup, rattail haircuts—and I doubted they were locals.

I went to the men's room, and by the time I returned Bob had struck up a conversation with them. I supposed he was telling them about our day, about the trip that stretched out in front of us, but the music was too loud for me to hear anything. When Prince's "Little Red Corvette" came on, the blonde and Bob went off to dance.

"So, are you tourists, too?" I asked the brunette.

She shook her head and said something I couldn't make out.

"What?" I said.

She stuck her face in my ear and told me she was from Seiverville, which we'd passed on the way in, about fifteen miles north of the Heartbreak Motel. Her name was April Mae Clemens, her friend's was Darla something, and they both worked as back-up singers for the Ronny Lee Umphlette Review, a country-and-western show that performed daily at a nearby tourist attraction. I also learned that she and Darla still lived at home—so much for a place to stay—but Bob and I ended up dancing and talking with them until closing time anyway.

Somewhere around last call Elvis's "Burning Love" came on, and afterward I mentioned that we were planning to visit Graceland in a few days.

April Mae Clemens smiled. "You know, I got a theory about Elvis. I don't believe he's dead. Not old Elvis. The way I figure it, he just got tired being in the spotlight, being in the public eye every waking moment."

"Well, sure he did," I agreed.

"You wait and see. He'll make a comeback one of these days. But right now, the way I figure it, he's used all his money and bought up Jamaica. He's probably livin' in a big old house down there—bigger than Graceland Manor, I'll bet—and paying everybody off so they don't tell on him."

April Mae Clemens invited us to see them back up Ronnie Lee Umphlette the next day and promised free passes if we got there early enough. We'd probably be there, I told her, knowing we wouldn't. We have places to go, I thought. We have to see if Elvis is really dead.

3
American Trilogy

Because of the inherent uncomfortability of automobile seats pressed into service as beds, I woke up near dawn. Three inches shorter, Bob slept on in the back seat as I worked to extricate my head from underneath the steering wheel, desperate to go outside and take a piss. Once free, keeping the door open so as not to wake Bob with a rude slam, I made my way to the back of the nearest building, stopping every few steps to groan, stretch and crack miscellaneous vertebrae.

I admired Bob for having thought to park here, at the fringe of Pigeon Forge, on the lot of an auto body shop that seemed to be dedicated to the repair of hulking cars left over from the Johnson Administration. Since none of the adjoining Furies, LeSabres or Galaxies looked more in need of repair than El Basurero, there was no danger of getting nabbed for vagrancy. Zipping up, I smiled, certain we'd happened upon a method of finding safe lodging anywhere in the contiguous United States.

I started the car and drove vaguely south. We were back on the interstate—I-75, bearing down toward Chattanooga—by the time Bob awoke and clambered over the front seat.

"Next stop?" he said.

"Guess."

He looked puzzled.

"As far as I'm concerned," I said, "this is the kind of a trip where you look for a sign and be guided by that."

Bob read off the first billboard on our right: "Ruby Falls."

Ruby Falls is no doubt featured on more billboards and barnroofs than the combined roadside oeuvre of the members of Gatlinburg/Pigeon Forge Chambers of Commerce—and over a far greater territory. I've seen them in Florida and Oklahoma. A friend of Bob's claimed to have seen one in upstate New York. But along the corridor of Tennessee superhighway, their numbers increase exponentially toward Chattanooga—as do those of Ruby Falls's crosstown rival, Rock City—so that from the corporate limits on, it's possible to see Ruby Falls signs so close together that their shadows overlap.

"My mom used to work parttime at Ohio Caverns," Bob said.

"I've been there," I said. Near Bellefontaine, Ohio, about ten miles from where Bob grew up, there's a collection of tourist attractions pretty much unknown to anyone outside the Buckeye State, of which Ohio Caverns is one. The others are Zane Caverns, Mac-O-Chee Castle, Mac-A-Cheek Castle and—in Bellefontaine proper—the first stretch of concrete pavement in America (1891). I learned about all these from Mrs. Clarke in seventh-grade Ohio history class, and subsequently conned my parents into a weekend trip to Bellefontaine, for which I received some sorely needed extra credit. "Maybe your mom was my tour guide."

Bob nodded. "I used to get in free. I've never paid to tour a cavern."

Halfway up Lookout Mountain I sailed El Basurero into a parking slot, where we changed shirts—a wise decision, Bob announced, for anyone about to be confined in a small underground space with a large group of strangers. In honor of Ruby Falls we each wore the gaudiest shirts we'd brought: mine, an old bowling shirt; Bob's a thrift-shop job exploding with purple flowers.

Inside, once Bob saw that our journey into this storied cavern would set him back $4.50, he scowled and shook his head, heading for the giftshop to think it over.

Inexplicably I began to sneeze, again and again, caught up in a bizarre and uncharacteristic allergic fit that prompted nearby parents to gather up their children and eventually sent me to the men's room in search of a tissue. Bob followed along to see if I might die. "You should," I said between sneezes, "be happy to pay that money."

He looked unconvinced. "For $4.50 we could buy just under four gallons of gas and drive for almost sixty miles."

Our trip was well underway, I thought, pissed off both that I had to blow my nose with a coarse brown paper towel and that my traveling companion was displaying alarming, early signs of being an intractable, joyless skinflint.

"Are you going to live," he asked. "Is there anyone you'd like me to call? Can I have your album collection?"

"It's not that much, $4.50." I shook my head,

happy I hadn't sneezed for a while. "Look. You wouldn't go to Disneyland and expect to get in for free. This is America. Spending money isn't just fun—it's patriotic. Any good American would pay good money for the privilege of spending good money."

"People talk so much about 'good' money," Bob mused. "As opposed to what, I wonder?"

I blew my nose a final time, cured as abruptly as I'd been afflicted.

Apparently convinced, Bob paid the price of admission, and we boarded a crowded elevator to plunge down through 260 feet of rock "without a crack or crevice," according to the recorded voice that welcomed us, speaking in the same deep, melodious tones as the narrator of junior-high sex education filmstrips. "The fresh air in the cave remains a pleasant 58 degrees all year."

"My mom used to tell people that," Bob whispered.

Our tour guide, Amanda, had us introduce ourselves by hometown, a friendly touch that also supplied straggler insurance to twenty smiling tourists preparing to traipse single file through the core of a mountain. As an extra measure, Amanda told Memphis, the last person in our group, to bring up the rear.

"Roger, Amanda," he called.

"I thought he said he was from Memphis," Bob said under his breath. "Where's Roger?"

"At the end of the line," I said. "Aren't you paying attention?"

We paused near a back-lit lucite box that illuminated a flashing map of the very cavern in which we stood. Amanda pushed a button on the box's side and the Voice of Knowledge returned to present to us tourists the story of Ruby Falls.

Near the turn of the century, a group of Indiana businessmen formed a company—complete with stocks and investors—to sink an elevator shaft into the large cavern that existed below us, presumably drilling for minerals. After months of blasting and digging, corporate officer L. B. Lambert happened upon a tiny opening, scarcely large enough for him to wriggle through. After several hours he returned to camp exhausted and filthy, raving about the spectacular underground falls he'd found. That night, accompanied by his wife, Lambert again slithered hundreds of yards through the narrow cavern. Mrs. Lambert, legend has it, was as impressed by the falls as L. B. had been, and as a token of his affection, he named the falls for his wife. Her name, of course, was Ruby, and what L.B. had struck was tourism.

"Well," Bob said, exasperated. "Well. Ruby baby."

"'Ruby Baby,' the Drifters, Atlantic Records, 1956."

"1955," Bob corrected.

"I wonder if she ever worked as a truckstop waitress. Every Ruby I ever knew worked as a truckstop waitress. Chewed gum. Dentyne."

"How many Rubys have you known?"

"None," I admitted.

The tour filed downward.

"Are you still with us, Memphis?" Amanda called.

"Yes, still back here."

Just then trusty Amanda explained the difference between stalactites and stalagmites. "You can remember it like this," she said. "Stalactites are tight to the ceiling and stalagmites just *might* get up there someday."

Bob grinned. "Mom told people that, too."

Next they turned off the lights, exposing us to a darkness so complete that we felt compelled to utter our "oohs" and "ahhs."

Once light was restored to our world, we came upon the first marked limestone formation, Cactus and the Candle. These two stumpy lumps hardly fit this description, which sent Bob into apoplectic envy of the person whose job it was to name these formations. I had to agree that affixing arbitrary names to stony lumps was a job for which he would be ideally suited, so long as the world was prepared for dripstones named Unctuous Slugs from Hell.

In fact, few of the formations seemed rationally named. Nevertheless, behind us, Kansas City told his grandson that, sure, he could see the Holy Family in that cluster of white stalagmites—why just look, there's three of them, ain't there? Kansas City's grandson looked unconvinced, probably having learned in school the tale of the emperor's new clothes.

We could hear the sound of falling water for quite some time before Amanda herded us into the dim chamber that housed Ruby Falls proper. Several amber-lensed spotlights shone through the water as we were directed around the perimeter of the pool at the bottom of the falls. I was hoping that Bob wouldn't take this opportunity to upbraid me for talking him into this. He would've had the moral footing to do so, since the only remotely remarkable thing about Ruby Falls was its underground location.

Four speakers on the walls behind us came to life, throbbing with forgettable classical music. The Voice of Knowledge welcomed us to Ruby Falls itself. Additional banks of lights ignited the water, turning the thin falls the color of a hothouse tomato. The Voice then told us that no one had ever discovered the origin or destination of the water passing before us.

As North America circled the pool, countless flashcubes augmented the wall-mounted reds and yellows. Children begged their parents for coins. Kansas City's grandson threw a handful of pennies toward the roof of the cavern, grinning as they splashed down. The boy was refused when he asked Kansas City for more money, and turned his back on Ruby Falls.

Aside from different angles of formation that from the front had been only borderline miraculous, there was little to see on the way back to the surface. Had I taken this subterranean adventure with my family, by now Mom would have begun to complain about her feet. Lacking that diversion, we made light in the dark.

Mrs. Toronto asked her husband for the time, concerned about when they might reach Nashville later that afternoon. Mr. Toronto wasn't certain, beset with worries about Daylight Savings Time and Central Standard Time. When he asked me for help, I had to confess that neither my friend nor I owned a watch. Ahead of us, Kansas City reported that it wasn't too awful far past nine.

"What's that in dog years," Atlanta asked, and most of North America chuckled—travelers happily unconcerned about the clock and quick to deride a tight schedule.

About halfway back, the path split. Bob started to sing "You take the high road, and I'll take the low road . . ."

Without any encouragement, Kansas City, Mr. and Mrs. Toronto, several of the Mid-Atlantic states and I joined in.

"For me and my true love shall never meet again," we sang, full of voice and weak of tune. "By the bonny, bonny banks of Loch Lomond."

Amanda brought us to a halt near the elevator shaft, thanked us for visiting and enjoined us to return. I looked around our group, and for one giddy moment felt lucky to have been in a place with so many people from so many places, no matter how frivolous our collective mission.

The price of our admission also included access to an observation deck atop a vine-smothered tower. Once we arrived, the Voice again greeted us, calling the leafy vista before us "the Grand Canyon of the Tennessee." As Grand Canyons go, it wasn't much, though I guess no Ohioan ought to be snide in his critique of topography. As the Voice explained this area's appeal to the native Indians—a bend in the Tennessee River which, to them, supposedly looked like a moccasin—I tried to identify the five states this view was said to offer. Tennessee, Georgia—and that was as far as I got. The standout landmarks were Chattanooga and gray ribbons of three different interstate highways: I-24, I-59 and the mighty I-75.

Eventually the Voice named Tennessee, Georgia, Kentucky, Virginia and both Carolinas—and further suggested that we could see the air over Alabama. The whole concept baffled me. I never understood why we could see Kentucky, Virginia and South Carolina—each more than 100 miles away—and only the air over Alabama, a mere 16 miles away. While Bob and I debated this moot point, less pretentious tourists pointed their cameras toward Alabama and let their shutters click and whir.

"Thanks for coming to see us," the Voice concluded. "Stay as long as you like, then have a safe trip and enjoy your vacation."

We opened the doors of El Basurero and waited for the hot air of the outside to cool the hotter air of the interior. Like every other car in the lot, El Basurero had a cardboard "Ruby Falls" placard affixed with aluminum clips to its front bumper.

Bob fished two beers from the tepid water of the cooler.

"It takes a big man to admit he smells," I said, rolling my beer can across my forehead, then—unbuttoning my shirt—across my chest.

"Never," Bob said, "let it be said that you're not a big man."

"Thank you."

"So," Bob said. "You want to go to Florida?"

"Sure. As long as we can find some place to shower first."

And with Bob at the wheel, we two Ohio boys entered the deep South, on the most perfect interstate highway I'd ever seen, windows down, beers open. I took off my shoes and dangled my feet out the window, savoring at excessive volume the shoebox of cassette tapes we hadn't yet grown sick of. For no reason we began to talk like one-dimensional caricatures of rednecks.

We laughed and laughed, out of place and obtuse, alien to a part of the country we would never understand, admitting defeat by slowing below 55 only to gas up and to take a shower in the bath house of a state park that had been established, a sign said, during George Wallace's first term as governor.

4
The Sun Sessions

That Bob had never been to Florida seemed wonderful and incomprehensible, as strange as if he'd never eaten at a McDonald's. But when we crossed the Alabama-Florida border, Bob didn't wake me to share the moment. Head slumped against the car door, I slept until a particularly rough Pensacola railroad crossing sloshed the melting ice in our otherwise empty cooler.

"What time is it?" I said, repositioning my head. "Are we there yet, Dad?"

Bob stared ahead. "I've been driving around Pensacola for half an hour. It's not quite midnight."

By then I was asleep again. Bob continued to drive all over Pensacola, including two trips across the huge, arching bridge that leads to Pensacola Beach. I woke up every minute or so, but then abruptly fell back to sleep, often in the middle of sentences. I gathered—after a very long time—that Bob was scouting places where we might park the El Basurero Motor Lodge for the evening.

To kill time we stopped in a bar named Molly

McGuire's, which had the same cramped, back-slap-
ping, throw-up-on-your-shoes atmosphere as your typical college bar, the kind of place I have a real weak-
ness for. These were only minor variations between
this and any number of Ohio bars where I'd disgraced
myself: a benign, and ignored, coffee-house singer;
eighteen-year-old Navy burrheads in the place of nine-
teen-year-old fratboys; and walls covered with $1
bills. Navy guys jostled one another for next dibs on
the stapler and the black magic marker, eager to become immortal by signing their name to United States
currency and affixing it to a tavern. I ordered gin and
wished I wasn't too sleepy to get drunk and run amok
with a quality stapler. Bob ordered tonic.

I'd fallen asleep when two short Marines tapped
me on the shoulder. "Hey you," the shorter one
snapped. "Stand up."

Bob looked at me, raised an eyebrow and
shrugged.

I stood. "Howya doin'?"

"Will you—I mean, can you stick these mother-
fuckers up there?"

The other Marine held out his hands, stapler in
one, two signed dollars in the other. "Up on the roof,"
he said, pointing.

"The *ceiling*, asswipe," said the first to his pal.
"Up on the goddamn ceiling, he means."

I stood on my chair and, barely able to reach,
stapled their currency above their heads.

The two little Marines thanked me and shook
my hand, then embraced one another and carried on
as if they'd just scored a winning touchdown.

"No prob," I said.

This innovation precipitated a flurry of activity
as, all around us, members of the Armed Forces
staked out their respective patches of ceiling.

I reached for my wallet.

"Don't even think about it," Bob said. "If you do, I'll rip it down and keep it."

I didn't actually go to the beach until I was fourteen years old. I'd seen both the Atlantic and the Pacific many years and many times before that, but despite three trips to Florida my family had never really gone to the beach. We stopped there, but we never *went* there. We went to St. Augustine and Cape Kennedy and Disney World and Busch Gardens and the Daytona Motor Speedway, and to be honest, it never even occurred to me to ask my parents if we could spend a day at the beach.

But by the time I was fourteen, like most fourteen-year-olds I found my family impossibly freakish, and I didn't see why we couldn't take vacations like other people did. After suffering months of my cajoling, Mom and Dad relented to a week at Myrtle Beach.

On our first day, Shari got a blistering sunburn, Mom fainted from heatstroke, Dad tore out the seat of his swimming trunks and I slashed the bottom of my foot on a broken Pepsi bottle.

Then it got worse. Shari insisted on walking around with this dorky umbrella, much to my mortification. Mom, who doesn't tan, stayed inside the motorhome reading historical novels. Dad spent the days metal detecting on the beach and being followed around by a troupe of munchkins who wanted to know if he was really going to keep that rusty butter knife.

For my part, I wore a floppy sunhat and one sweatsock, even into the ocean. The sweatsock was meant to protect the gash on my foot, which became infected and oozed yellow pus, and the sunhat was meant to protect my vanity. Just before we left, at the Greater Northwestern Ohio Aquatic Conference Championships, I got carried away by an adrenalin rush (and an offer of $50 cash) and I shaved my head. Though I did well at the swim meet, I hadn't counted on how difficult a self-conscious adolescent would find looking like a chemotherapy outpatient. So I wore the sunhat every waking moment, until school started and the vice-principal said he'd suspend me unless I took it off.

During college I went south for spring break each year, my first vacations without Mom and Dad and Shari. Those four vacations were identical to the ones everyone else took, and only later did they seem boring.

Not long past dawn, we ate at a Waffle House behind which we'd just slept. Bob continued to pinch pennies, ordering only hash browns and chocolate milk. I opted for a real meal: eggs, bacon, grits, toast, juice and coffee. "I'm getting a taste for grits," I said when the food came. But our waitress saw me top my grits with sugar, and for a moment I thought she might call the police.

We finished eating and drove to the beach. Since the battered benchseats and curtainless windows of El Basurero had again forced us into an earlier start than any sane person would want, we were among the first dozen vehicles in the several-acre beachside parking lot—probably the first not belonging to employees of oceanfront weenie stands. Seagulls swooped down to pick at the trash scattered across the blacktop. "Those birds," I said, shaking my head, "are just pigeons with good press agents. And pigeons are just rats with wings. To think hobby painters waste perfectly good canvas on them."

"You know, you wouldn't say that if you were a Mormon," Bob said. "Let's get some supplies. I hadn't exactly planned on going to the beach. All I have is a towel."

Pensacola Beach had the same assortment of beachwear and party stores that you'd find around any of America's public beaches. Carry-outs stock a good selection of styrofoam coolers, overpriced domestic beer and baseball caps with sayings like "The only way they'll take away my handgun is to pry it from my cold dead fingers." Most restaurants, no matter how pricey, serve people in thongs and wet swimming trunks. Surf shops cater to both tourists and surfers: $500 surfboards lean unceremoniously against inflatable Godzilla rafts. Even the gas stations stock postcards, tanning ointment and sunglasses, although, after you look through a few racks, you get the disquieting feeling that the same wholesaler supplies every last retailer. The people behind the counters are friendly, but their eyes seem a bit glazed over, as if the inexhaustible whir of interchangeable tourists requires more attention than they care to spend. I can't say I blame them.

Bob and I walked two miles down this strip, searching for the cheapest beer, the biggest bag of ice and the silliest four-color postcard. Tanning products seemed to cost the same from surf shop to T-shirt shack, as if the Pensacola Beach Chamber of Commerce had imposed price fixing. Bob deferred to my three years of lifeguarding experience, and in a pleasantly cluttered place called the Sundry Store we chipped in for a bottle of the same stuff I'd used on the job. Bob spent 91 cents on postcards with poems about dogwood, magnolia blossoms and sand dollars, then asked the jocular old woman at the cash register if she had any particular favorite.

"Oh, I guess I'd be partial to the dogwood one," she said, flipping through them. "That's the only one I ever read, but of course I'm biased, being born again and whatnot." This postcard featured the legend about the dogwood's guilt at having to serve as lumber for Christ's cross, which is why the dogwood no longer grows large enough to be used for crucifixions and why each of its blossoms contains a tiny cross.

"Makes sense," Bob said, counting out pennies. "That *is* a good one."

It wasn't yet nine o'clock when we got back to the main beach: an hour too early for peak tanning or beer drinking, too sunny and public for quality sleeping. Bob spent an hour at a picnic table writing postcards while I found a pay phone and made two calls. The first, collect, woke up my friend David Gretick in Chicago; he accepted the charges and I told him we'd be dropping by in five days or so. The second, on a WATS-line, was to Laura at work. She took care not to say she missed me already, but she seemed to. "We confirmed the menu for the reception," she said. "Canneloni."

"Terrific," I answered, probably without requisite enthusiasm, looking out over the ocean, watching the first few sun worshippers spread their towels and tune their radios.

"Is that okay with you?"

"It's great. Really. I mean it." I knew I was letting her down, and I knew she was indulging me. I told myself I loved her for this, but wondered if I would've respected her more if she'd insisted on my help. Or maybe I'd have felt suffocated. We were supposed to get married the summer before, but the vast machinery of the wedding plans had scared me off. That, along with the fact that I'd been an immature, self-absorbed weasel.

"I wish I were with you," she said. "I mean, I didn't mean to say that. I understand. I just mean with the beach and all. Listen, I really have to go."

I walked back to the car, frightened whether I missed her enough.

"I thought *you* had the keys," I said. "You drove."

"You had them last," Bob hissed. "I gave them to you when you got your towel out of the trunk."

"I gave them back. I'm *sure* I gave them back."

Bob pressed his face to the passenger window. "Well, they're definitely not in there. Not locked in, I mean."

"I really did give them back, I'm sure of it. Don't you remember? I said I didn't have any pockets in these shorts and that you ought to hold on to them."

He made a slow lap around El Basurero. Suddenly, rapidly, the parking lot was filling. "Well." He remembered. I *had* given them back. "Well."

"You wouldn't happen to have one taped to the underbelly somewhere or anything like that?"

Bob scowled. "If we lost the keys . . ." His voice trailed away. The sun shone on the blacktop. There was no wind.

"Not an extra in your wallet?"

"Derrick Watts has the only other key—the only copy there is. My mom doesn't even have a key." Derrick Watts, a friend of Bob's, had no telephone and was, at that moment, in Youngstown, Ohio.

As we retraced our steps, back past Beachwear

Bonanza and its ilk, scanning the ground as if we were employing invisible metal detectors, Bob insisted on mumbling the worst-case scenario. We could, of course, break into the car with a coat hanger, but we'd need keys to get into the trunk—where most of our things were—or to drive anywhere. This afternoon Bob would write Derrick Watts a letter, asking him to please express-mail the key, care of General Delivery, Pensacola Beach, Florida. Until it arrived—for a week or so—we would roam the streets at night and sleep on the beach during the day, trying to avoid nasty vagrancy arrests.

Bob ran through this unpleasant litany in a flat, even tone, clearly resigned to spending the next several days in misery or in jail. He was still too dazed to be angry, but walking beside him I feared the moment when he realized this trip had been my idea, that were it not for me he might otherwise be painting houses back in his hometown. In that context, it would have done little good to remind him that he, after all, was the one who lost the keys. "I'm sure we'll find them," I said with the synthetic optimism of those too cowardly to face the alternative. "They have to be somewhere."

Painstakingly we stopped everywhere we'd stopped before, crossing the streets at precisely the same places. We asked for the lost keys at every cash register, hoping a kind, conscientious soul had turned them in.

Bob said he wouldn't be surprised if some curious tot had found them and decided the shiny keys and their electric-blue gelatinous fob might make a nice beach bauble.

Before he'd convinced himself this is what had happened, and before the knots in my intestines had curdled my breakfast, we found them, in the Sundry Store. Bob had left the keys on the counter while he'd counted out the pennies for his postcards. For two hours they'd sat undisturbed on the corner of that counter. The born-again clerk hadn't even noticed them.

"Gracious," she said. "Y'all sure are lucky they didn't walk off. These are good people around here, though."

His back to her, Bob was already halfway out the door.

"We sure are," I said, following. "Lucky, I mean."

Though I knew better, from then until late afternoon I was prone, oiled and shirtless. I drank beer and slept, relieved our keys had returned to the fold and delighted to lie down someplace where my legs could be fully extended. The girl-watching was borderline inadequate, although I did enjoy a conversation with a perky Loyola College junior—a native Puerto Rican named Vicki, up from New Orleans for the weekend—whose synopsis of the World's Fair made me want to go.

On the radio a station advertised itself as "The Rock 'n' Roll Voice of the Redneck Riviera." This was followed by a spot for a Pensacola nightclub—located someplace called Saville Row—which, for four nights only, was featuring a prominent Elvis impersonator.

Not long after noon, Bob said he'd had enough sun. When I told him I hadn't had nearly enough, he put on a T-shirt and went for a walk.

I called him a wimp. What prototypical tourist could face himself if he hadn't, at least once, been properly sunburned?

Charred and nauseous, I searched my suitcase for loose-fitting clothing. Bob revealed himself as a true friend, resisting the great temptation of saying he'd told me so. Food, I decided, would help: I hadn't eaten since the Waffle House that morning. Although Bob had planned to save money by fasting, he agreed to go grazing with me at a Wendy's all-you-can-eat salad bar. "My dad always used to say you could make a lot of money writing a book that listed every all-you-can-eat restaurant in America," I said.

In line, we noticed that the prices were about 10 cents more expensive across-the-board than at the Wendy's back in Oxford. "Maybe the ones in Ohio are cheaper," Bob mused, "because they're closer to the home office in Columbus."

A Navy kid in front of us, with a crewcut so short his hair resembled gunpowder, turned and asked us if we worked in a Wendy's.

"No," I answered, startled. "We're just smart shoppers." He seemed confused by that, so I added, "We're on vacation, a real low-budget vacation."

"Oh," he muttered. He placed his order—two doubles, loaded up with condiments, and a bevy of side orders. "You know," he said to us, "if you ever decide to go in the Navy, go into Search and Rescue. It's the hardest to get into and the second hardest training, after the Seals." He smiled beatifically. "But it's worth it."

The three of us went through the salad bar at the same time, and as we contorted ourselves to reach under the sneezeguards for garbanzo beans, the Navy kid briefed us on the local bars, slipping in references to his sexual conquests in each, most recently "the ugly bitch" he'd pried off his neck that very morning. "I hope I didn't leave my ID behind. I haven't seen it all day." He had the odd habit of nodding at everything he said, as if trying to convince himself.

Bob smirked. "Maybe you'll hear from her again, in, oh, nine months or so."

I laughed.

"Jeez, I hope not." Our sailor was horror struck. "I already have one of those."

"Oh God," Bob said. "Sorry about that."

I could hardly believe I'd laughed at this sad caricature of a swaggering man of the world.

"It's damn expensive, having kids," he said, nodding and going to join two of his brothers-in-arms near the front window.

"You think he really has a kid," I asked Bob.

"Wouldn't surprise me."

Hunched over my ovoid styroplate heaped full of chemically preserved greens and radioactive cheese, I knew food wasn't going to help much. I went to the bathroom in search of a stall where I could take off my pants, blow air on my blistered thighs, clutch my queasy belly and grunt or groan for a while.

On one of our family vacations I contracted chicken pox. The trip—a week-long Smoky Mountain jaunt—is best remembered in family annals for that illness (edging out the beard my father grew, a favorite of the kids, but not of Mom's, and it was short-lived). But since then I hadn't been sick on vacation, until now—and in the men's room of this Pensacola Wendy's, I could think of nothing worse.

One of my more traumatic childhood memories involves an inner-ear infection my mother contracted one year when we were coming back from Colorado. Just over the Nebraska line, she grabbed the side of her head and screamed. Shari and I thought she was dying. Fortunately, Dad had bought into the CB craze, so he was able to get on the squawkbox and, with the help of a woman whose handle was Ogallala

Sue, find the location of the nearest hospital, where miraculous eardrops were prescribed.

After a half hour in the john, I felt marginally better. Bob smoked, waiting for me to return and eat my salad. He acted just like a friend should, I thought: no impatience, and no "are-you-okay's."

At the window table, the brothers-in-arms ordered the Navy kid from his seat. While he pumped out countless push-ups, they hurled at him all manner of dehumanizing taunts, to which he invariably replied, "Determination and motivation." I wondered where his child was, if there was a child.

Pensacola's Saville Row, its exterior amply festooned with wrought iron, turned out to be four or five bars with different motifs, all along the same side of a block, linked by interior halls and stairways. One $3 cover charge provided admittance to any of the establishments.

The largest was the rock 'n' roll bar, Rosie O'-Grady's—which, along with the previous night's Molly McGuire's and half the other businesses in Pensacola, extended the city's odd abundance of Irish names. Rosie O'Grady's could well have been in Indianapolis or San Antonio, Milwaukee or Dayton: a standard-issue heartland dance-rock club complete with neon, two tiers, five video screens and several million televisions. The crowd seemed vaguely collegiate—interesting haircuts, inscrutably blasé, wanters of their MTV, both sexes sporting multiple earrings.

Bob was hit on, more or less immediately, by an auburn-haired legal clerk and former Cincinnatian named Jamie who bore an uncanny resemblance to a young woman Bob had been greatly smitten with a couple years earlier: an auburn-haired premed student and present Cincinnatian. This was the kind of stupid, implausible coincidence that makes people fall in love in bars.

I spent the night far from the dancepit, huddled in the corner of the bar with shy computer nerds and befuddled farmboys. Exhausted and again nauseous, I sat back and allowed the night to roll over me in a tide of cigarette smoke, lingering tanning oil and junk culture. Bob found me near last-call, and I wondered if he'd let Jamie go off alone because he had no place to take her, because his car, even, was my lodging, but I was too beat to dwell on that or ask him about it.

Sunburnt and dissipated, we slept where we had the night before, amongst battered cars. The last thing I remember was Bob mumbling something about us having missed Saville Row's Elvis impersonator.

"Maybe it's the wrong day," I said.

5

It Happened at the World's Fair

Once Interstate 10 dumped us smack-dab in the City of New Orleans, we passed dozens of signs for the Superdome and the World's Fair, but none for the French Quarter.

"It's the oldest part of the city, right?" Bob said, and, without waiting for an answer, added, "Okay, so that means it's down by the river."

"Sounds reasonable. So how do we get to the river?" I'd been to New Orleans once before, a Christmas vacation with my family when I was a freshman in high school and too young to drive or pay attention to the roads.

"Take Business 90, there," Bob said. "See—'Exit 2 Miles.' That'll take us downtown, down by the river. The Mighty Mississip'. The Big Muddy. Old Man River. Father of the Waters." He seemed pleased as hell to be able to rattle off these epithets.

I drove El Basurero through downtown New Orleans, almost to the river, and took a left when Bob said, "Turn left—I think I see some streets with French names."

This put us on the edge of the French Quarter;

a profusion of wrought-iron railings and a gentle feeling of familiarity. When we passed Jackson Square, I knew exactly where we were. "Let's just find a place to park," I said, "then we can walk around. We're bound to run into Bourbon Street eventually."

I've seen too many movies intended to pervert the cliché of Southern hospitality—movies where people lacking drawls wind up sodomized in Mississippi jails—to be eager to ask questions in the South, especially questions that peg me as a Yankee tourist. Consequently we spent two hours looking for Bourbon Street. Tired and about to give up, we turned a corner, and I didn't need a sign to recognize Rue Bourbon.

Concrete and steel barriers close it off from automobile traffic, allowing people to walk right down the center line, gaping at the higgledy-piggledy juxtaposition of businesses. Which is all any first-time visitor could hope to do, since I doubt there's any stretch of real estate in America that so thumbs its nose at modern zoning. Adult bookstores abut teddy-bear shops, world-famous jazz clubs abut bondage supermarkets.

The people milling around on Bourbon Street were at least as diverse as the businesses lining it. Two bearded men, their skin painted gold, handed out flyers good for a free drink in a nearby strip joint. Fathers swiveled their necks as mothers picked up the pace and applied hands over the eyes of overly curious children. Black kids carrying boom boxes spun around and slapped one another on the shoulder, laughing conspiratorially. A bored, helmeted cop leaned against a doorway, working a toothpick from one side of his mouth to the other, staring at the sky. A bag lady with a pet duck sat on the curb, either weary or drunk or both, feebly waving a plastic cup at passersby. Three painfully beautiful young women escorted by their mother or chaperone sailed past, smiling exhibits of skilled orthodontia as they joked with one another, their heads tossed back in explosions of laughter, wonder and tumbling curls. Finally there was us, a couple of hungry, sunburned and road-gritty graduate students from rural Ohio.

Near the end of the cordoned-off section, Bourbon Street abruptly became stranger and seedier. Most people see or *feel* this blocks in advance and turn around, heading back toward parked cars and comfortable hotels, but tired and stupid and curious, we stumbled ahead. The streetlights dimmed in deference, and the crowd dwindled to less than a dozen stragglers: bored, lost or actually in search of that dark streetcorner where a young evangelist in a red flannel shirt flourished a Bible and a zippered case overflowing with papers and pamphlets. A few feet away a cluster of winos were collapsed in a heap, the conscious ones passing around a bottle in a brown bag. Across the street an enormous gay bar's second-story balcony was packed with men who chatted, hugged and kissed while they taunted the preacher. He hung tough, giving them measure for measure, leafing through the Bible, pointing at pages he never seemed to recite from, raising up a clenched fist and inviting the Good, Sweet Lord Jesus Christ to smite these devils, to bring His considerable wrath down upon their heads like a colossal, thousand-ton claw hammer.

A wino pulled himself upright, walked to the evangelist and whispered something to him. In return he received a stack of pamphlets. The evangelist then directed his attention to the curious onlookers: three disinterested hookers; an outraged, balding holdover from the '60s; three very amused rednecks drinking Pearl beer; Bob and me. I was afraid he'd single me out, hollering and waving his fist in my face, commanding me to praise the Lord. But suddenly, a plastic cup full of ice came swooping down from on high. The evangelist spun around, faced the balcony and lit into the tale of Sodom and Gomorrah, thumping his Bible, spitting fire, breathing brimstone.

A black kid, no older than fourteen, came down Bourbon Street toward us. He carried a box as big as a suitcase, and Herbie Hancock's "Rockit" blasted out of its two huge speakers in a fury of hip-hop robotics. He was walking with his eyes closed but must've sensed something, because he abruptly opened them, cocked his head and took in the scene. He flicked off the music and stood there bewildered for about a minute. Then he grinned, flipped his machine back on— louder this time—and did a two-step as he twirled around, heading back toward civilization as we know it.

Bob and I followed him down Bourbon Street until he stopped to talk to a friend, the cashier at the Jewel Street Cabaret. A sign invited us to see Johnny Rusk's tribute to Elvis *and* Elvis's 1969 Mercedes-600 limo, all for one low price.

After an hour spent searching the French Quarter for a half-decent place with $3 all-you-can-eat shrimp Creole, we finally settled on the Gumbo Inn, a small restaurant three blocks from Bourbon Street with reasonable prices, a roomful of smiling customers and a brass plaque on the outside conferring historical significance upon the building.

It was Sunday night, but the Gumbo Inn was packed. The maitre d' asked if we'd mind sharing a table. We didn't, and he seated us next to two women, obviously a mother and her teenaged daughter. The mother had finished eating and was self-consciously dainty as she sipped her Manhattan; the daughter stared at the table, poking at her jambalaya.

Bob and I ordered, and I asked him if he knew what time the World's Fair opened in the morning.

"Oh, so you're going to the faya?" the mother broke in. She patted down the back of her new-wave haircut, then shrugged. "The faya's faya. Just faya. Wouldn't you say so, honey?"

Her daughter didn't even look up.

"I mean, talk about your expensive. They want $3 for an ice cream, can you believe that? But it's not bad. It's, you know. It's faya."

I looked at the girl, whose eyes were still fixed on her plate. She was hardly breathing.

"Now, the New York World's Faya, that was—" The mother paused, drawing tiny circles in the air with her highball glass, searching for the right word— "that was magical. Just magical. Dawn's father and I went at least ten times, driving all the way from Lakewood—Lakewood, that's in Jersey—all the way from Lakewood, ten times we went." The woman was almost singing. "That was when we were just dating, Dawn's father and I. The faya, that faya, was, well, it was a magical kingdom is all I can say."

Dawn jumped at the mention of her father, and I realized that her parents were divorced, that she lived with her father, and that her mother was trying to cram weeks of interaction into a brief vacation. Going to a World's Fair seemed a sweet gesture, given her parents' courtship, but one that was obviously lost on Dawn. I tried to imagine a tactful, subtle way of encouraging her, but couldn't.

After our food came, Bob and I somehow got into a mild argument with the mother about when World's Fairs are held. I knew the Knoxville fair was in '82—I'd seen a bumper sticker attesting to this fact only a few hours before on I-10—and was pretty sure Seattle's was in '69 and Spokane's in '77.

Bob nodded. "They're sort of sporadic. Some city decides, 'Hey, we're going to have a World's Fair,' and then they draw up some doomed municipal bonds and that's that."

Frowning, the mother unequivocally informed us that World's Fairs were held every four years, just like the Olympics, national presidential elections and leap year.

"Maybe you're right," I said, aware that dragging this argument out would only aggravate whatever rift existed between her and her daughter.

Dawn remained mute, and, when their bill came, her mother snatched it up. "Let's go, Dawn," she said, then to us: "You boys have a good time now."

In front of the empty display window of the Bourbon Street Woolworth's, an obese, blond-bearded man in a raggedy once white dinner jacket blew "Amazing Grace" on his battered saxophone: slow and mournful, peppered by tortured-waterfowl notes that made the hymn even more achingly sincere.

Bob pointed at the coins and bills in the guy's cheap red-velvet-lined case. Just then a man wearing a $500 suit and a $100 haircut walked by the saxophone case and, without breaking his brisk stride, tossed in a dollar bill. "I'll bet he makes five bucks an hour, easy," Bob said. "All he needs is a dollar every 12 minutes."

We stood toward the back of the small crowd,

far enough away that we wouldn't feel too guilty about not contributing to the cause. People who live in rusting Impalas shouldn't throw coins.

Apparently Bob was right. After no more than three minutes, at least ten people had flipped money into the case. The man breathed heavily, made an extended show of smoking a Lucky Strike, wiped his mouth with a hand towel, and then, sliding his lips tenderly over the reed in a wet little kiss, started into "Amazing Grace" again. Surely this wasn't the only song he knew. But this time he blew more forcefully, and the squawks were in new places. His case continued to fill. After watching him smoke another Lucky, wipe his mouth and start "Amazing Grace" yet again, Bob and I headed up the street.

Half a block south another small crowd had gathered, this time around a whipsaw of a man sporting a huge afro, an ill-fitting polyester tuxedo and square wire-rimmed glasses with clumps of tape on the temples. For a while he arranged long, tangled cords around a footlocker and a small amplifier, then pulled out a black ventriloquist's dummy—dressed, of course, just like his owner, including the tape on the glasses—and took a seat on the footlocker. The dummy pointed out the inadequacies of observers' breasts and penises, and the excessive size of their asses, while the ventriloquist, after each insult, put his hand over the dummy's mouth and shushed him. This got laughs, but only from people who hadn't been singled out. About thirty people had gathered in a wide circle, each one moving gradually toward the rear.

Certain that my penis would soon become the object of public derision, I inched backward and bumped into a young woman behind me. "Excuse me," I said. "I'm just trying to get out of his line of sight."

"Same here." She laughed. "That guy's awful, isn't he?"

She wasn't alone in reaching that conclusion, since the crowd had started to peel away. By now the ventriloquist was trying to wring laughs out of teasing kids with candy. I tapped Bob on the shoulder and did the *let's go* wiggle with my eyebrows. "I think we're clearing out," I said to the woman. "Being made fun of in front of a crowd full of strangers isn't exactly what I had in mind."

She laughed again. "Me neither." She tugged on the shirt of a woman next to her, and the four of us wandered off. When the sax player started "Amazing Grace," the ventriloquist's dummy shouted at him to shut the fuck up.

The woman's name was Angie, and she worked as a switchboard operator at the Downtown YMCA; her friend, Min, was entering Long Beach State University that fall as a creative writing major. We made our introductions as we walked down Bourbon Street, and—whether by design or coincidence—I sort of paired off with Angie and Bob with Min. Angie seemed thrilled to hear about the trip, both where we'd been and where we planned to go. She loved travel herself. "It's sort of my hobby, I guess," she said. "I got two big maps on my wall at home. On one I color in the states I've been in. The other one—it's bigger—I use that one to draw in the routes I took. Both maps are pretty blank, I guess, but I'm workin' on it." She told me she was hoping to visit Min in California in the fall and her cousin in Washington, D.C., for Christmas.

Two guys fell in alongside us and struck up quick conversations with the two women, ignoring Bob and me. They obviously knew Angie and Min, and asked them to go someplace I couldn't quite make out over the din of Bourbon Street. Min looked like she wanted to go; but Angie said they were busy. The guys' eyes widened, then they frowned and walked away, shaking their heads.

Angie and Min were black, and of course I noticed that right away. But it never occurred to these guys that we might be with them, because they were black and we were white. If the races and sexes were reversed, if I'd been in Angie's place, I haven't the slightest idea what I'd have done.

We all four wound our way through the side streets and main streets of the French Quarter, stopping to buy sodas from a machine in the Farmer's Market, and ended up on the levee of the Mississippi, sitting on wooden benches on a new boardwalk. Angie told me there'd been a lot of work done to spruce up the city—especially the tourist district—for the expected flow of visitors that summer. "The fair's not doin' what people expected," she said. "The people in charge of it are idiots." But she told me that the fair itself was worth the price, and—when I told her Bob and I were going to go the next day—Angie said she had the day off, and we agreed to go together. "You could show us around," I said.

Bob and Min sat a few feet away and seemed well into their own conversation, but Angie and I didn't need any help. She told me about her job, about how homeless people called her every day demanding free housing and, when she tried to explain that the Y had neither the space nor the funding for that, asking her, "Girl, don't you know what the 'C' in YMCA stands for? It stands for Christian." I told her more about our trip, and how we had been living in El Basurero. She told me that the police in New Orleans really don't bother people too much and that we'd probably have no trouble finding a side street to call home. She and I discovered we had similar attitudes about auto repair: an attitude that, over the years, had provoked much consternation on the part of each of our fathers;

an attitude made up of equal parts poverty, laziness and utter mechanical ineptitude and disinclination. "You should put gas in it," I said, "and it should just go." Angie wasn't even convinced that you ought to have to put gas in it.

We stared across the river at blue-collar Algiers, where Angie lived, and tried to figure out what it was about rivers and campfires that can captivate people for hours. At first Angie said it was because they're both so peaceful, but then she laughed. "That's stupid. It has to be something more complicated than that." Though I agreed, I couldn't come up with a theory. We sat in silence for what must've been a long time, witnessing the steady progress of tons of silt and millions of gallons of water—some of which, I noted, might have flowed underneath El Basurero four days before, when we'd crossed the Ohio River in Cincinnati.

"Fire and water," she said finally. "It's fire and water, doing their job in constructive ways. The fire gives off warmth, you know? And the river, well, the river can be used for transportation. But when you watch them, you can imagine a forest fire or a huge flood. And that's what makes them so great to watch. You can see fire and water at peace. Under control. But you know they could kill you, too."

It was pushing midnight when Angie and Min said they had to go home. We got up from our board-walk benches and headed past Jackson Square. Bob and Min were laughing easily, and it was obvious Bob was well past his layer of aloof and studied reticence.

I guess it was because Angie and I were caught up in our own conversation, but before we were 20 yards down the street we noticed that Bob and Min weren't right behind us. We turned around. Min stood facing three elderly black men on a park bench, and I could tell from her hand on her hip and the way she moved her head in staccato jerks that she was angry. She wasn't yelling, though, and I couldn't hear her. Once Bob and Min caught up, I started to ask him what had happened, but he closed his eyes for a split second and gave a tiny shake of his head.

On the way to their car, Angie and Min stopped to exchange small talk with a group of friends. I turned to Bob. "What happened back there?" I whispered.

"You didn't hear it?"

"Hear what?"

"Well, right as we walked by, the guy on the bench looked at Min and said, 'Three hundred years of slavery for this?' And she got mad at him."

Angie and Min called goodbye to their friends, and we walked them the rest of the way to their car. Angie gave me her phone number and told me to call her tomorrow, to set up where we'd meet.

"Goodbye," I said when we arrived at her white Dodge.

"See you later," Angie said. "Tomorrow."

Bob and I made our way back to El Basurero, past the bearded saxophonist still playing "Amazing Grace." The street ventriloquist was gone. We sat on the hood of the car, telling each other what we'd talked about, marveling at how many worlds we were away from Oxford, Ohio, at how far we'd come in four days. And then we sat in silence, drinking in the muggy air and studying the wrought-iron railing with weary detachment.

I knew then I wouldn't call Angie. We would've had fun, no doubt. But I was afraid of too much. I'm engaged, I rationalized, that's all there is to it.

We piled into El Basurero and spent the night on a New Orleans side street, parked alongside a white marble mausoleum.

Other than the small amount of information I'd gotten from Angie and from the woman in the Gumbo Inn, I had only three preconceptions about the 1984 Louisiana World Exposition (its official name):

A. The souvenir shops we'd seen all over Louisiana, filled to the rafters with their usual blizzard of trinketry—glasses and T-shirts, Frisbees and bumper stickers—all adorned with the likeness of the Fair's official mascot, a pelican called Seymour LeFair.

B. The numerous newspaper accounts of how much money the Fair was losing, how it might be something of a financial pelican around the necks of Louisiana taxpayers for the next decade.

C. A rave review in *Time* magazine, talking about how the whole Fair was one gigantic party, a pan-cultural feast of music, food, dancing, food and food—written by a man so elated by the joys provided by his expense account that his poor heart could take no more and, honest-to-God, committed fatal myocardial infarction just as he finished writing his article.

Preconception A was amply borne out inside the Fair's much-statued gates. Official Souvenir Stands were carefully located so that no visitor to the Fair could at any time be more than 30 yards from one, and nearly all of the national pavilions had their own Official Souvenir Stands, so there was every opportunity to plunk down traveler's checks for stuffed koala bears, Canadian history books, or (as Bob did) a little red pin with a gold horse on it—the Official Symbol of Chinese Tourism. You could even buy a videotaped tour of New Orleans and the World's Fair hosted by Ed McMahon, the last five minutes of which consisted of an interview between Ed and the purchaser of the cassette. For instance, Ed will ask, "So, are you having a good time here at the 1984 New Orleans World's Fair?" and you answer, "Sure, Ed. Now tell me, when you fill out your tax form, what do you put in the 'occupation' box?" and then, through the magic of videotape, some technician splices the two together.

Liggett and Myers, sponsors of the Quality Seal Amphitheater, even had the Official Cigarettes of the 1984 World's Fair, sold in Official Souvenir Stands and given away behind the Quality Seal Amphitheater by a woman dressed as a pack of cigarettes. Bob grabbed a couple packs, but would later throw them out the car window, complaining that they tasted like grocery bags shredded and rolled into cigarettes.

Preconception B proved equally accurate; the Fair's failing finances cast a shadow as long and dark as the unfinished Mississippi River bridge that towered over the United States pavilion: the center part apparently finished but, spookily, joined to neither shore. Attendance—according to *USA Today* the very day we went—was running at about half what the Fair needed to break even, so every Monday had been designated "New Orleans Day," when locals were admitted for half price in hopes they'd make it a habit. A good fifth of the exhibits weren't finished, mostly those of Third World nations. Admittedly this might have been intentional; as a soft-sell appeal for financial aid, Belize's pathetic lone easel of black-and-white photos was hard to beat.

As for Preconception C, the rave in *Time,* I'll say only that we would've had more fun if a national magazine had picked up *our* tab. As it was, once Bob saw the ADULTS: $15 sign, he vowed not to eat anything all day.

Standing in a large, dark, round room, we were abruptly surrounded by Lee Iacoccas, five of them, each on pentagonal screens two stories high and talking, in synch, about the Chrysler Corporation, its remarkable comeback and its commitment to the future.

This spiel was similar to the TV ads in which Iacocca strolled through a showroom in much the same way that Sherlock Holmes would've walked through a parlor full of suspects immediately before revealing the solution to the crime: a man eminently in control of his world. But the effect of these Goliathan Iacoccas-in-the-round was more like being confronted with a brilliant and benevolent Oz eager to unveil his vision of a better world.

The movie that followed Iacocca's introduction was edited in a frenetic, music-video style and loaded with gee-whiz designs, inventions and manufacturing techniques, but it could not compare with the iconic zing of the man himself. If Iacocca decides to enter politics and can stage his campaign commercials in-the-round, America will have her first king.

The only aspect of the Chrysler exhibit that wasn't overwhelmed by the presence of its president was a sharkfin-shaped attachment that will be available on 1989 Chryslers. The fin is an antenna, really, that connects a little TV screen inside the car with a communications satellite in outer space. This option, at the flip of a switch, will show you where you are, no matter where in North America that happens to be, right down to the city block or county road. If you're lost, the computer will tell you the fastest way to get found. If you need to know the fastest or the most scenic route from New York to, say, Terre Haute, no problem. There are no codes to learn: a little directory in the right-hand corner lists the programs, and all you have to do is select one.

I remember the fights my parents would have when Dad took the wrong turn and got us hopelessly lost, and the fight I had with Laura when, absorbed in a book, I allowed her to get us lost in downtown Atlanta, and the tense moments Bob and I have had debating the fastest route from Gatlinburg to Chattanooga.

Imagine the fin atop the pitted roof of the seventeen-and-a-half-year-old Chevrolet that brought us here. I asked the woman demonstrating the map-of-tomorrow what it would cost. "About a thousand dollars," she said, "maybe less."

A pittance, this, when you think in terms of friendships, marriages and families saved from ruin.

I'll never attend another World's Fair, not as long as they have themes. Actually, themes would be okay if they weren't always so pathetically serious. "Food: Come and Eat Lots of It!"—now that's a good theme. Or, "Rides and Music: Fifteen Bucks and Worth Every Cent!"

But the thing is, World's Fair themes are supposed to be educational, and the best exhibits are likely to resemble the kids' wing in a science museum—lots of buttons to push, lights to light up and special effects to say "wow" over. And given the choice between dropping fifteen dollars on a thoughtful afternoon at a well-run science museum or on a sweaty Saturday at Disneyland, I'm in line for the Matterhorn every time.

The theme for the 1984 Louisiana World Exposition had a fancy science-fair name—"Fresh Water as a Source of Life"—that boiled down to "Our Friend, the River." Even if you're Mark Twain, a little of this can go a long way. Most of the English-speaking countries were savvy enough to add buttons, lights and other special effects: the huge movie screen in the Canadian pavilion, for example, or the 3-D flick in the USA's. But most other countries treated the theme with utter solemnity. The Chinese exhibit, filled with a fortune in ancient tapestries and furniture, was rendered insufferably boring by a lengthy explanation of the Chinese aqueduct system. Soon enough, the history of Egyptian rivers flowed over the history of Brazilian rivers, which in turn flowed over the history of Mexican rivers—until I ached for a simple roller coaster.

The corporate exhibits, with the singular exception of Chrysler's, took the theme just as seriously, even if they had to force it. Union Pacific Railroad showed a film called "Railroads: Rivers of Steel." In the Great Hall, a 35-foot latex model of a beating human heart bore the name, "The Human Circulatory System: Rivers of Life." Even NASA, in an exhibit next to the space shuttle, offered a lengthy description of how they got Enterprise to New Orleans. That's right, they put it on a barge in Mobile and sailed it through the Intracoastal Waterway and up the Mississippi!

Buttons push, lights flash, tourists yawn.

At ten P.M., a reduced admission of four bucks—what amounts to a cover charge—allows you into the bars on Fulton Street, and if you've been at the Fair all day, you can stay for free.

We'd heard there was a new-wave band at Sally's, an Australian-theme bar. The band was just finishing up their set when we got there, though, and it was hard to tell exactly what kind of music they played. The lead singer, a tiny woman with glittery mascara, wore a heavy-metalesque leopard-spotted spandex jumper; the keyboard player and the drummer were nouveau New Wave with skinny neckties and haircuts no 9-to-5 boss in America would allow; and the guitar player, except for the diamond stud in one ear, could've passed for a rising young paralegal. Everyone in the bar was white.

I thought about buying a beer, but Bob screwed up his face. "Here?" he asked. "Even *Miller* is three bucks."

"Well, I'm hungry. How about a sandwich?"

He shrugged. "You can. I don't want anything. I'll watch, though."

Whoopee, I thought, and headed outside.

On Fulton Street a local R & B station had parked a farm wagon sideways across the street and was blasting Afrika Bambaataa and the Soul Sonic Force at a huge crowd packed around a half dozen breakdancers. Bob and I stood on tiptoe, craning our necks for a glimpse of a perfectly executed moonwalk, centipede or head-spin.

I looked around and noticed we were about the only white people when an archetypal tourist family (complete with stretch fabrics and oxblood cordovans) happened by, probably a good facsimile of what my family must have looked like on most of our vacations. They stopped and stared, as if this street party were an avant-garde film's depiction of Christmas on Mars, then walked away shaking their heads, looking for a place that served red beans and rice in white Styrofoam bowls, a place where a toothy LSU student in period costume would play Stephen Foster songs quietly on his banjo and leave them in peace.

Then a skinny white kid wriggled his way into the center of the circle. About fourteen years old, he was dressed in an expensive breakdancing uniform (multicolored sleeveless T-shirt, black parachute pants, red-white-and-black hightop sneakers) that smacked of suburban mall. He stood there, nervously shifting his weight, looking for an opening. The breaker in the middle was about the same age, a black kid just finishing an astonishing run of moves: he planted his right hand on the street and spun his whole body around it, then sprang up and slapped the newcomer on the shoulder.

The white kid flashed a trace of panic, then smiled a stagey smile and hip-hopped his way to the center of the street. The crowd hardly reacted to this desegregation, apparently willing to see what the kid could do.

He ran through most of the basic breakin' repertoire and, when another dancer joined him in the center, had no trouble playing off him, picking up the nonverbal signals just as a batter eyes his third-base coach. But his steps seemed mechanical, as if he'd locked himself in his bedroom for a month with a Grandmaster Flash record and a how-to manual. There was no street in anything he did.

When he finished, there was a sprinkling of polite applause, but even I felt myself looking at him as some sort of cultural carpetbagger. I could just see him getting in a cab later tonight and heading to a comfortable townhouse in the University District, while most of the people he'd danced with would take the ferry across the Mississippi to workaday Algiers.

Bob decided to go back to Sally's and watch the band for a while.

"I'm starved," I said.

"Suit yourself," he said, and he was off.

I went into a little cafe across the street. Submarine sandwiches are called Po-Boys in New Orleans, and that sounded perfect to both my stomach and my wallet. I walked to the counter. "I'll have a—" and I suddenly imagined what the black dialect variation of "poor boy" would sound like coming from the tongue of someone who grew up in a county in Ohio where no black people have ever lived. "A sandwich. You know, a—" and I mumbled—"Po-Boy."

I took my sandwich to the cafe's patio and ate slowly, listening to the music and the cheers. People laughed and wiggled and joked as I watched it all, from behind.

6
Elvis
for Everyone

Outside Winona, Mississippi, on a whim, I suggested we take a detour to Tupelo, birthplace and boyhood home of Elvis Aaron Presley. "I think we need to see Tupelo before we see Graceland," I said. "After all, Elvis did."

"Is there anything there," Bob asked. He'd been driving since we left New Orleans that morning, piloting El Basurero as fast as he ever drove—about 58— up I-55: at first a concrete ramp suspended a few feet above the bayous and eventually a typical Southern interstate dissecting the floodplain. "Any tourist things?"

"I think there'd have to be. There's just too much money to be made for there not to be."

Bob drove in silence for a while. He clearly didn't want to go, but I still thought it was a good idea, even though it would force us onto Mississippi 8, which stood to be a quaint road and, as such, a bit out of whack with our conception of the trip. Bob lit a cigarette with the car lighter. "How far out of our way is it?"

"Take this exit," I said, turning around to retrieve the map from beneath a pile of fruit pie wrappers, dirty clothes and World's Fair effluvia. "I'll check."

Bob obeyed, irritated but ostensibly pliable.

When I found the Mississippi map, I knew immediately I'd bollixed things up. There were no direct routes to Tupelo, and it would take at least two hours, maybe more, since an orange sign warned of an impending detour. But we were committed, I thought, for better or worse.

Worse, since El Basurero had a flat.

I'd never changed one before. The whole time Bob worked on it, the only thing he said was, "Here, hold this," as he handed me a fistful of lugnuts. The shoulder was too narrow to pull entirely off the road, so I used that as an excuse for something to do: I stood behind El Basurero and waved pickups around us.

I'd have felt better, I think, if Bob had yelled at me, if he'd accused me of using our friendship to coerce him into coming along in the first place.

When he spoke again, it was to tell me to help him put the tire on the wheel.

I did, then said, "Let's just forget Tupelo, under the circumstances. Let's just get back on 55 and that way we'll get into Memphis while it's still light out."

We got back into the car and did just that.

Near Memphis International Airport, I-55 intersects with Elvis Presley Boulevard. Graceland is clearly marked, both on roadsigns and our sorry map, which indicates "Graceland" with a red square, and no further explanation. No "Home of Elvis Presley." None necessary, apparently.

Throughout the trip I looked on the map for other famous homes that were deemed similarly self-explanatory. Even Monticello was appendaged by "Home of T. Jefferson," and only Mount Vernon spoke for itself. This, then, seems to be a distinction cartographers have reserved for an odd pair of American originals: the Father of Our Country and the King of Rock 'n' Roll.

The salient difference, of course, is that Mount Vernon is a national monument, visited by a few hundred thousand people a year. Graceland, visited by millions, is an industry.

By the time we made our way to Graceland, it was dusk. There was no attendant at the parking booth, and a sign explained that the remaining tours were full. We resolved to return first thing tomorrow. "Let's go to Beale Street," I said.

Shaded by maples in the middle of a Beale Street park that bears his name, there stands a statue of W. C. Handy, Father of the Blues. A few blocks away is a statue, about the same size, of Elvis. Handy is surrounded by three blocks of restored buildings: clean, ornate, neon nightclubs, daiquiri shops and tourist information centers. Like Bourbon Street, the street itself has been shut off to traffic. Curiously, even on a beautiful Friday evening, the revamped Beale Street is far from the teeming hub of blues and raucous nightlife I'd expected. From reading James Baldwin and William Faulkner, from a jazz-and-blues-appreciation class I took in college, I'd hoped for something magical, but Beale Street and its establishments were all but empty.

In refurbishing the street, the city went too far,

removing the soul of the place along with its layers of decay. What remains might be historically accurate, much as a movie set would be, but is nevertheless too antiseptic to ever again pose as the place B. B. King once called "college for blues men."

On the blocks between the statues of Handy and Presley lie dozens of boarded-up and burned-out buildings. These blocks will soon go the way of their neighbors: coming-soon signs and properly displayed building permits warn of restaurants, boutiques and trendy lofts to come. But as they are, in their advanced stages of dilapidation and ruin, they provide a stark contrast to the nexus of new neon to the east and the downtown business district to the west, an anonymous collection of glass boxes.

Alongside a bank building, a 12-foot Elvis, bedecked in bronze fringe, looks even farther to the West.

We slept in the parking lot of a Howard Johnson's in the 3400 block of Elvis Presley Boulevard. Bob had wanted to look for another garage specializing in the repair of huge, battered American cars from the '60s. But I convinced him of HoJo's advantages by noting its proximity to Graceland, its poorly lit rear lot and my overwhelming desire for immediate sleep.

"How many nights since we've slept anywhere else?" I said upon waking barely past dawn, cranking down the window and groaning with pleasure and pain as I extended my feet skyward. "Let's see: Gatlinburg, Pensacola, Pensacola again, New Orleans, and now—"

"Five nights," Bob muttered from the front seat.

"The last time I slept in a bed was, I reckon, during the Ford Administration. Ever since then I been livin' in this here Chevy. Acourse I don't have to tell you that."

"Nossir, you surely don't."

On the west side of Elvis Presley Boulevard, across from Graceland itself, the parking lot borders a dozen giftshops and a fenced-in compound containing Elvis's tour bus and his two airplanes. On the tail of the larger one, a jet, underneath a parallelogram-shaped American flag decal, was a logo in gold letters: TCB with a lightning bolt underneath.

Next to the compound was the loading area for the white raised-ceiling vans that transport twenty tourists at a time to the front porch of Elvis Presley's home. Though tours didn't start until nine, and it couldn't have been long after that, we were assigned to tour group D, which meant there were a few hundred folks ahead of us. Bob raised an eyebrow and affected a pained look when he saw the tour would cost us six bucks. He'd known about this trip for months, I thought, and besides, he'd just inherited a little money. I wasn't sure I could take three more weeks of his whining about money.

Bob finally paid and, while we waited in the adjacent giftshop, he considered paying even more. "Isn't this great? An Elvis ashtray. I think I'll buy it. For bad taste, pink flamingoes don't have a leg up on Elvis ashtrays."

"Well, wait until after the tour," I said. I wanted to buy a piece of Elvisobilia myself. "We're up next, and you aren't going to want to carry that around all day."

Bob laughed and set it down. "Okay, we'll come back. Right after the tour."

The van's eight-track tape player treated us to "Rock-a-Hula Baby" as the driver welcomed us to Graceland, shuttled us across the street, and told us we were among the 6,000 visitors who tour the mansion each of the 360 days that it's open. Six thousand people. Over two million a year.

The front of the house is not gaudy, and the house itself is of the minimum size necessary to qualify as a "mansion." Its architecture is neither Antebellum Southern nor Hollywood glitz; in fact, with its gray stone walls, black shutters and four modest white columns, Graceland could easily be mistaken for a dormitory at a Midwestern women's college. It could, except for the steel bars covering all the windows.

On the front porch our lovely tour guide Kelly—wearing, like all Graceland employees, a blue pinstriped shirt, navy chinos and perfect hair—told us that in 1957, at the age of twenty-two, Elvis purchased Graceland and the 13.8 surrounding acres from Dr. and Mrs. Thomas Moore "for one hundred thousand dollars cash." That was a good year for Elvis. For precisely half of 1957, he had the #1 record in America: first "Too Much" (three weeks), then "All Shook Up" (nine), "Teddy Bear" (seven), and "Jailhouse Rock" (seven). I found it hard to imagine: I was now the same age that he was then, and I was living in a Chevy.

"There is still a family member living in the house today, Miss Delta Mae Presley Biggs," said our guide. "That is Elvis's aunt, on his father's side. She's been living here since 1967, when she became a widow, and according to the . . . um, er . . . at the invitation of the estate, she is welcome to live here as long as she pleases." She was a bit flustered by her flub of the canned speech, but few of our group noticed. Most of us were consumed by frantic gawking, irrationally expecting—on cue—an appearance by this frail old woman returning home from Piggly Wiggly.

Our group didn't seem significantly different from a random sampling of twenty tourists plucked from the World's Fair or Ruby Falls. They wore shorts, mostly, and a few middle-aged men embarrassed their families by sporting dark socks and street shoes. I suppose I expected people to be carrying red roses to lay across Elvis's grave and boxes of tissues to sop up the tears they planned to shed.

Kelly explained that no flash photography would be allowed inside, due to its deleterious cumulative effect on drapes and upholstery. No movie cameras or tape recorders, either. "We also ask that you refrain from sitting, leaning or touching anything in the home. It is still a private residence, and we'd like you to show the same respect as you would in any other private home."

As a few thousand more people would do that day, we filed solemnly into Elvis Presley's private home.

We acquired a new tour guide in the dining room—a Kelly-clone with a singsong delivery that sounded remarkably unlike human speech. We learned that the dining-room table, built for six, usually accommodated a dozen guests at each meal; dinner tended to be served between 9 and 10 P.M. The pattern of Elvis's everyday china was Buckingham. "Elvis always sat there at the head of the table, not because he considered himself the man of the family, but because that chair gave him the best view of the TV set you can find in your left-hand corner. Now, we do believe that Elvis was an avid TV watcher, and this is just one of fourteen sets located throughout the home."

In the living room we saw a custom-built 15-foot sofa and 10-foot coffee table and framed photographs of certain family members that were said to be favorites of certain other family members. Beyond the couch were stained-glass partitions decorated with peacocks, Elvis's favorite bird. "At one time here at Graceland, Elvis had about fourteen of these peacocks running around, until they scraped the paint off Elvis's Rolls Royce. Then Elvis gave them to the Memphis city zoo."

A short, pretty, sixtyish woman next to me chuckled. "Fourteen televisions, fourteen peacocks." She elbowed me in the hip. "That's some kind of coincidence for you, isn't it?"

I agreed.

At the far end of the room was a concert grand piano, "twenty-four-carat gold leaf, inside and out," an anniversary gift from then wife Priscilla.

"Why, that piano's worth more than the whole neighborhood Elvis grew up in," the woman said. "Don't you think you'd lose your grasp on reality if you had a piano like that?"

Again I agreed.

She introduced herself and shook hands with Bob and me. "I'm an Elvis fan from way back, you know," Chloe said. "My students told me about him back in 1955. I was teaching in Minnesota then. Microbiology."

Except for the mirrors in the entry hall and along the staircases—installed in 1974, "when Elvis's decorator, Mr. Bill Eubanks, said that they gave the home a more spacious look"—the first rooms were fairly subdued: whites and grays, forgivable flourishes of royal blue and gold.

At the bottom of the stairs a new escort told us that "tourists do not go into the upstairs area due to personal family reasons, but I can tell you what is located there. Elvis's bedroom—above the living room/music room area—Lisa Marie's bedroom, dressing rooms, bathrooms, and also Elvis's office."

"Upstairs," Chloe interjected. "That's where Elvis—"

"Passed on," interrupted the guide. "Yes, ma'am."

"What room was that in?"

"We don't know for sure. None of us has ever been up there. No one really goes up there anymore. Miss Delta Biggs lives downstairs, through that door over there."

"So," Chloe persisted, "you don't know what it looks like up there?"

"No ma'am. Almost no one does. I'm sure you can understand."

In the basement we saw further work of "Mr. Bill Eubanks." The TV Room was done in bright yellow and blue—the exact shades used on Cub Scout uniforms. Displayed on one wall was the TCB symbol we'd seen on the tail of the jet; this was Elvis's personal logo, which stood for "Taking Care of Business in a Flash." The room also contained a wet bar, a jukebox, several televisions, and an eclectic record collection, a mixture of gospel, blues, rock 'n' roll and Dean Martin, who the guide cited as Elvis's favorite singer. We also learned that the televisions were almost always in use simultaneously.

"Dean Martin?" Chloe said. "I could never *abide* Dean Martin."

The Pool Room featured 750 yards of pleated fabric, affixed to the walls and ceiling to resemble mutant wainscoting. We were assured that the rip on the pool table was not made by Elvis—"a good pool player whose favorite games were eight ball and rotation"—but by a friend attempting to execute a trick shot. Above our head was one of several surveillance cameras installed throughout Graceland in the early '70s.

Sources say the basement was the King's favorite portion of his castle.

Nicole welcomed us at our next stop: "The den, or Jungle Room." Added to the house in 1965, this was the only room Elvis decorated himself—and it fulfilled my worst fears with a (now broken) waterfall, rampant ferns, sofas and chairs covered with pseudo-animal hide and supported by arms and backrests into which animal faces and paws were carved. Because the ceiling and walls were carpeted with mottled green shag, the acoustics were good enough to allow two lackluster albums—*Moody Blue* and *Live from Elvis Presley Boulevard*—to be recorded here. Elvis also ate his breakfast here in the Jungle Room, at a polished cypress coffee table.

When Lisa Marie, Elvis's daughter, was a toddler, she enjoyed napping in a huge, barrel-shaped chair in the corner. "Lisa Marie," Nicole said, "is now sixteen. According to her father's will, when she reaches the age of twenty-five, she will inherit this estate in its en-*tire*-ty. It's all being held in a trust fund until then."

On our way outside Chloe asked me what I'd do if I were Lisa Marie.

"It'd be great, I guess, to have the whole world love your dad so much. But I think I'd boot the tourists."

She agreed. "You're right, though. It would be flattering. People in my hometown hated my father. He was a traffic judge."

Somewhere, Lisa Marie might've already made her decision. In 1993, we'll all find out. Then, perhaps, two million people a year will have to wander through someone else's private home.

Outside in the carport we saw a portion of the Presley motorpool: motorcycles, a Dino Ferrari, two Stutz Bearcats and a 1955 pink Cadillac—a gift his mother never used because she didn't know how to drive. We tourists could have our pictures taken in a fringe-topped pink Jeep (which Elvis drove in *Blue Hawaii*) or on one of Elvis's snowmobiles. Because of the lack of snow in Memphis, Elvis had the skis removed and go-kart wheels installed. On the snowmobile I leaned to the left to imitate a severely banked curve, then Bob and I asked Chloe to take our picture in the Jeep. She snapped two, as we took turns driving.

"Do you want your picture taken, too?" Bob offered.

"No thank you," she said. "I find it just a bit ghoulish, to be honest, sitting on vehicles only because Elvis might've once sat on them." She handed me my camera. "But I do suppose they'll make a good souvenir for you boys."

The Trophy Room had been forged out of a garage-sized building in which Elvis housed his sprawling slot-car track. Now it's a museum. The building's former pastime is represented only by six slot-cars and four pieces of track.

In the first of three rooms, memorabilia was arranged chronologically to create a timeline of Elvis's life, starting with photos of him growing up in Tupelo and recording his first singles with Sun Records, continuing through his draft notice, a pile of his movie scripts, three Grammies and paintings of his favorite horses, concluding with a large lucite box stuffed with telegrams received on the occasion of his death. "Thank heaven," Chloe muttered, "there's none of the drug material." Several of us nodded in agreement.

The second room was devoted to his gold and platinum records, of which there are hundreds. I'd expected this to be more interesting than it was, but gold and platinum albums all look about the same, even when some of them are Brazilian and Norwegian.

In the third room: miscellany. Here we learned that Elvis was six-four in his stocking feet and wore a size 12D shoe. Here we saw a replica of his wedding cake, his acoustic and electric guitars, and several pounds of jewelry, including solid-gold car keys and a gigantic TCB ring. Display cases were packed with trophies, medals, keys to cities, and letters from fan clubs, martial-arts instructors and politicos (including Richard Nixon, Jimmy Carter and J. Edgar Hoover). One case contained ten of Elvis's guns and forty-four of his honorary law-enforcement badges, most of which were awarded for narcotics enforcement.

But the clothing is the soul of the room. The

first suit displayed is the black leather affair a svelte, dangerous Elvis had worn in the famous 1971 Singer TV special that had been a reaffirmation of his mammoth talent. The suits after that marked a descent into beads, buckskin and bell-bottoms. Fringe was a favorite accessory, until its excess began to promote Elvis's entanglement in microphone wire. Rhinestones gained favor next, reaching a peak with an enormous, bejeweled cape—never used because it weighed too much for Elvis to lift.

Alongside the exit is an unfinished jumpsuit, the color of the deep end at a municipal swimming pool. Elvis was scheduled to wear it onstage August 17, 1977, but he died the day before. I looked past it, back toward his snazzy wedding tux, his leather jacket and his platinum record for "Suspicious Minds," then across the room to his guns and his slot-cars. The contrast between what the man achieved and what he'd come to be was so stark and so immediate that I knew I could never again consider Elvis Presley's death in any way premature.

We walked into the sun and out to the memorial garden, where we joined a few lingering tour groups at the graves of Elvis, his stillborn twin, his mother, his father and his grandmother—all arranged in a semicircle, with Elvis in the center. Flowers were strewn across the bronze tablets marking the final resting place of each Presley, though the graves of Elvis and his mother boasted more arrangements than the others. Few cried or made any sort of noise. People studied and photographed the inscriptions on the tablets. As she walked away from all this, Chloe shook her head and spoke to no one.

The van dropped us off back at the airplane holding pen, where I convinced Bob that despite the extra $3 admission, his trip to Memphis wouldn't be complete without the adjunct tour through Elvis Presley's private plane, the *Lisa Marie*.

This tour had its own giftshop, a smaller version of the one we'd already been in. Framed flight documents filled the walls—Elvis's first flight, his last, various flights to and from noteworthy concert appearances.

"God, then it must be real," Bob said, pointing to one of the frames.

"What must be real," I asked.

"This." Bob laughed and shook his head. "I just thought this was one of those apochryphal celebrity legends," he said. "You know, like George Washington and the cherry tree."

But there they were, the flight papers from a twisted journey Elvis commissioned on Groundhog Day of 1976, when he converted a mere hankering into an act that provided the world with a working definition for obscene wealth. Late that night, the King piled his entourage onto a jet and flew them to Denver, Colorado, for peanut-butter-and-banana sandwiches.

When the *Lisa Marie* touched down, it was greeted by a long, black limousine. A man got out, bearing big silver trays full of food readily available in every Memphis supermarket. Elvis and his lackeys snatched up the sandwiches and taxied down the runway. If we read the flight document correctly, the entire trip took fewer than five hours and required 42,000 gallons of fuel.

"He died almost exactly a year-and-a-half later," Bob said. "I'm guessing this is the sort of thing one might have to answer for."

A film we were shown before our trip through the *Lisa Marie* featured Elwood David, the pilot on that Denver excursion and part of the four-man flight crew that Elvis had on call at all times. David seemed tentative as he told the story of his most famous flight, relating the facts as if he were giving an affidavit that would imprison his King. "Sure enough, they were peanut-butter sandwiches and, um, Elvis insisted that the crew have some of his famous peanut-butter sandwiches," David stammered. "And, um, I'm not much one for peanut-butter sandwiches, but acourse I had to say it was the best peanut-butter sandwich I ever had."

Over strains of Presley's gospel music, our tour guide explained that Elvis had purchased the *Lisa Marie*—for nearly $1 million—to conquer his fear of flying, which had sentenced him to barnstorming in a converted bus like any number of Country and Western smalltimers. This speech was shorter than most of the ones in the mansion, though just as canned.

The plane was decorated in '70s velour and featured gold-flaked bathroom fixtures. Some of this we should perhaps forgive—few people in the 1970s wore or decorated with material that does not now seem embarrassing. So, to be fair, the plane wasn't half bad. The beds, sofas, recliners, wetbars and cardtables were arranged comfortably, and anyone who imagines some new carpet and upholstery can't help but covet the thing.

We poked around until the rest of our group had filed out. "I have a question," I asked the guide.

"Glad to answer it." She had beauty-pageant

hair, coated with enough hairspray to stay curly even on this hot Memphis summer day. She couldn't have been much older than sixteen.

"I mean—how do you listen to this music pumped in here every day? Isn't there times you get up in the morning and think you'd rather die than listen to Elvis?"

"Actually . . . no." She smiled, right at home on this plane. She would make a great stewardess. "You'd think that, but it grows on you. You start listenin' to it on your spare time, too."

"Oh, come on. You listen to Elvis in your *spare time?*" I consider myself a fan, but this hardly seemed plausible. And even if it *were* somehow plausible, it was incontrovertibly deranged.

"Really," she insisted. "You know, not all the time. But a lot of times you do. It's real easy to get all . . . hyped up. Like I said, it becomes . . . I mean, it grows on you."

Just out of earshot, Bob examined the King's VCR. I could hardly wait to tell him about this. "Don't be offended, but that's strange. You know, not what you'd think. Is that, uh, common among the guides?"

She nodded, though her hair stayed put. "It's that way with everybody. Even if you weren't an Elvis fan when you started workin' here, you start likin' it a whole lot more."

I almost asked her how long she'd been coached to answer that question. Instead, I chose a friendlier tack. "Do people ask that question a lot?"

"Yeah. We get asked everything, just about."

I caught up with Bob, who was teetering on the railing of the rear stairs, attempting to photograph the TCB logo on the tail. "Get this," I said, then told him about our conversation.

Bob snapped the shutter. "You know, I bet they have to go to classes. I bet it takes months to learn."

At an outdoor information booth we found a Graceland employee who was a little less doctrinaire. Ann, at least, lacked the glazed-over eyes and the sing-song voice of many of her co-workers. So I asked her. "There's a script, isn't there?"

She burst out laughing. "Well . . ."

"How long is it?

"Ninety-two pages," she confessed. "We all have to learn it." Everyone, she said, knew the speeches for every room, for the *Lisa Marie* and the memorial gardens, the works.

"So if I asked you the speech for the Jungle Room—"

"In my *sleep,*" she said.

We talked for a while, introducing ourselves, bemoaning the heat, flirting. She was a student at Memphis State—major undecided—and for her this was just a summer job.

"Would this be a good place to work," Bob asked. "See, we're English majors, so we have to look into any employment option."

Ann laughed. She laughed easily—a good audience. "It's, well, a job, let me leave it at that." Bob must've looked disappointed, because she added, "Well, the thing is, a lot of these people take it too seriously. And a whole lot were groupies and they just naturally gravitated to these jobs."

I told her about the stewardess.

"Yeah, we have a lot like her too. Terminally perky."

"Well," Bob asked, "do *you* listen to Elvis at home?"

She scrunched up her face. "Get serious. I don't even listen to him *here.*"

Past the booth walked two middle-aged parents who had suited up their little boy in a satin facsimile of one of Elvis' thunderbird-embroidered jumpsuits.

"Good lord," I said. "I hope that's not a common sight."

"It is," she said. "I think it's sort of mean, but we see a couple of those a week."

"Yeah." Bob fumbled with the camera, but couldn't get it focused in time to get a snapshot of the kid. "I believe you can be declared an unfit parent for that. It could at least provoke a mighty ugly custody battle."

We made small talk for a few more minutes, during which we learned that the blue-and-white-striped oxford shirts that all Graceland employees wear are purchased from the company for $9 apiece. Because Bob told her, she learned that Bob purchased his for a quarter at a thrift shop in Middletown, Ohio.

"Oh, now I know what I was going to ask you," I said as we were getting ready to leave. "Nobody ever gets to go upstairs no matter what, right?"

"Right."

"Nobody who works here, not even when you get started, as a part of orientation? Or, for a twenty-five-year pin, do they take you up and show you a closet? Nothing?"

"Not a thing."

"Curious?"

"Oh, yeah. Yeah. Real curious. All they tell us is what's up there. I don't even know exactly which room is located where, but I do know that Elvis's bedroom is located over the living room. I guess that's what I'd want to see most, his bedroom. Somebody told me once that nobody's been in there since he died."

"Really?" I asked. "No one?"

Ann smirked. "Ah, well. Probably not true. But you know, there's bound to be weirdness up there, don't you think?"

Bound to be, we agreed.

Primarily it was the air conditioning that drew us to the Graceland tourist information center, although that's not what I said. "Let's go in here. We're tourists. We need our adult minimum daily requirements of tourist information."

In the small carpeted room, Bob plucked brochures from a rack even more exhaustive than the one at the Pigeon Forge Heartbreak Motel, while I went to the counter and asked what else in Memphis warranted admission fees from thorough tourists. The woman smiled, produced a pink hi-lighter and city map, and commenced to circle nearly every attraction in Memphis, including something called The National Ornamental Metal Museum, featuring an annual event called Repair Days during which people could bring in any metal object for free refurbishment.

"Of all these fine things, which one do you most recommend?" I said, trying to keep her from turning the entire map pink. "We need something cheap, but otherwise, shoot."

She tilted her helmet of plastic hair a bit. "Way-ull. How about Mud Island? That's only three dollars, and it's pretty new. Most folks seem to really like it." She traced the quickest route with her hi-lighter. Mud Island, it turned out, was on our way out of town, on our way back north, on our way to Chicago and our first real shower in a week.

I thanked her and asked Bob how he was doing.

"All right. I want to go to the Ornamental Metal Museum," he said, handing me the brochure.

Two very pretty young women walked in and to the counter. Slightly younger than Bob and I, they were well tanned and wore Ray-Bans and the first normal haircuts I'd seen all day. I overheard them asking directions to Mud Island.

"We're going there," I volunteered.

"Okay," said the woman at the desk. "You all can just follow they-um."

"That'd be great," one of the women said. "We're terrible with directions."

It wasn't until we got to Mud Island that we remembered the ashtray. "Oh, God," I said. "I really hate to go all the way back there for an ashtray."

"Yeah. There was a whole row of souvenir places we didn't go to," Bob said. "Maybe they'll have an Elvis ashtray here. I'd think most souvenir establishments in Memphis would carry Elvis stuff." Bob stared out the window, his eyes on Arkansas. "As far as I'm concerned, I really wanted to go through all those souvenir stores."

"Well, why didn't you say something?"

The girls pulled into the Mud Island parking garage beside us. "Thanks!" they called as they jogged toward the monorail across the Mississippi.

"I knew you were determined to chase after them."

"I was not. It was just a whim. Anyway, *they* asked *us* to show them how to get here." I put on the parking brake with more force than might've been necessary.

"The road to hell," Bob said, "is paved with unbought Elvis ashtrays."

We rolled down the windows and sat silently in El Basurero. Bob smoked two cigarettes and I made myself a peanut butter sandwich. By now the bread had the texture and flavor of aged check stubs.

"Well, what do you want to do now?" I said.

"How much did the parking cost?"

"Two."

Bob took out his account book and duly entered the sum.

"We're here already," I said. "We might as well go."

"Did I ever say I didn't want to go? Are you done eating?"

Though there are steamboat rides, amphitheaters and river-artifact exhibits, Mud Island's main attraction is a scale model of the Mississippi River that is hundreds of yards long, sculpted in concrete and mind-numbingly detailed—complete with flowing water, proper to-scale depths, interstate highway bridges and stone-and-steel street maps of all major riverports. This seemed like a perfect attraction, both stupid and stupendous, equal parts history, Christo and hucksterism.

I loved it, and it made me realize how much I missed my family vacations. That Mississippi River model—audacious, unusual and educational—would've been a splendid day eater. We would have taken the official guided tour, walking slowly down the concrete, pausing reverently to ponder facsimiles of Minneapolis, Hannibal and the Everett McKinley Dirksen Highway Bridge. Mom would've explained who Everett McKinley Dirksen was. Dad would've been the straggler, daydreaming, remembering reading *Tom Sawyer* in 1948 in the waiting room of his father's outboard motor sales. I would've studied the sculpted Mississippi, fantasizing about carving out my own version in our backyard. Shari would have had to go to the bathroom. Mom would have stopped in the giftshop to purchase picturebooks of river lore; later—while we all ate soft-serve chocolate ice cream on the snackbar patio—she would have grilled Shari on details of the tricky delta passage south of New Orleans, which is in what state, honey? Now think.

That's what I wanted to do. But I had the wrong travel companion. Bob, worn out by "Our Friend, the River" from the World's Fair, wanted nothing to do with it. He began at the headwaters—somewhat delighted to find little Oxford, Ohio, depicted—then walked briskly downstream, pausing only in Cairo, Illinois, to take my picture while I did a Godzilla impression on the I-55 bridge (just a few hours before we would drive over its larger counterpart). After that, he handed me the camera and pointed to a bench where he said he'd wait.

I still wanted to learn something, so I listened on the far fringe of one of the guided tours. But after a few minutes, I glimpsed Bob, sprawled and exasperated on his bench, and I decided to appease him. We walked down to the Mud Island beach and, on the fortieth anniversary of D-Day, found rifle-sized driftwood and posed for photos designed to recapture the spirit of our fallen countrymen.

In vain we checked the giftshop for worthwhile Elvisobilia.

We walked back across the bridge to Memphis, back to Beale Street and the statues of Presley and Handy. I had hoped to see Sun Records, one of the few places on earth with a legitimate claim to being the birthplace of rock 'n' roll. "And I'll bet *they* have souvenirs." But at the Chamber of Commerce office we learned that Sun was closed for remodeling and, moreover, was twenty blocks away.

Minutes later, suspended over the river on our way to Arkansas, I riffled through the brochures Bob had collected at Graceland. One of them advertised "Elvis International Tribute Week," to be held the week of August 11, commemorating the seventh anniversary of the King's death. Among the special events planned were a karate tournament, a 10K run and a laser show choreographed to Elvis music.

7
Wear My Ring Around Your Neck

Bob pulled El Basurero off I-57 and into what had once been a Sinclair service station, now boarded up, with the FOR SALE OR LEASE placard every bit as faded as the dinosaur sign beside it. "Wake up," Bob said. "Drive."

"I'm awake." Sprawled across the backseat with my eyes closed, I'd been awake since Bob started singing along with radio gospel songs he didn't know in a fragile, insane falsetto, about 10 miles back. I sat up. It was the crack of dawn; I could almost hear it. "Time?"

"Drive," he said, his forehead resting against the steering wheel. "Drive or die."

"Where are we?"

"We are in hell," he said slowly. "We are on a road that should be named for Gerald Ford. We live as we dream, alone."

"How far from Chicago?"

"Hour, maybe two. We just passed Kankakee. Drive."

Bob slid over to the passenger's side, and after

thirty jumping jacks where the gas pumps used to be, I got El Basurero back on the four-lane.

"Shower," Bob hissed in the style of a B-movie psychopath. "Shower. I want a shower. I must have a shower." He started thumping his skull against the window. "Showers are good. Vote for showers. Put a shower in the White House. Put a shower in the back-seat."

The last shower either of us had taken was 1,791 miles behind us, in Oxford, Ohio. Four days before, in a New Orleans discount gas station, we each washed our hair in the men's room sink, did general dabbing with a soapy washcloth and changed clothes in honor of the World's Fair. Now, just south of Chicago, we wore the same clothes.

"We'll be at David's," I said, "in an hour. Less."

Bob began singing a medley of Osmond family hits in the style of Johnny Rotten. He never slept when I drove, ostensibly because he feared I'd abruptly fall asleep—but also, I'd wager, because he was certain his car was going to die and he wanted to be conscious for any poignant final explosions.

In Chicago we'd be staying with David Gretick, a friend of mine from Bryan, Ohio, who was a student at the Goodman School of Drama. His dorm room floor would mark the first building we'd slept in after a week in a Chevrolet. And that was too long. I was having a good time, but I needed some time to sleep and bathe and drink beer before Brad's wedding Saturday.

Chicago was just waking up as we lumbered down the Dan Ryan Expressway, and we managed to duck into the parking lot outside David's dorm—right under the Fullerton Street El platform—as rush-hour traffic began thundering down Michigan Avenue. The revolving clock at the corner savings & loan read 5:49. "Probably a little early to wake David up," I said.

Bob nodded. "I'm going to write some postcards."

"Me too," I said. "I haven't written Laura since the first day in New Orleans." But instead I climbed out of the car, walked to the back, hopped on the trunk, lit one of Bob's cigarettes with an Official Match of the 1984 Louisiana World Exposition and studied the passing trains, entranced as the right profiles of thousands of commuters shot by.

"I thought you didn't smoke," Bob said. "Where'd you put those postcard stamps?"

"I have no idea."

David Gretick's sister was my first crush. Kirsten and I were the only kids in Miss Cuff's 1966 morning kindergarten class who could read, but what had really won my heart was her speed on the kickball-diamond basepaths. My four-year-old heart threatened to outgrow its ribcage at the notion of a pretty girl who threw like a boy and knew the Cincinnati Reds' starting line-up.

Because she was so nimble, I never succeeded in dragging her behind the corner piano and consummating that crush in the usual Lincoln Elementary way, a quick kiss on the cheek and five minutes of uninterrupted giggling. This failed romance was soon lost in the recesses of prepubescent libido, forgotten until the ninth grade when we went to a Sadie Hawkins dance and two movies before she gave me the first just-friends speech I ever had to endure. Unlike every subsequent version, however, Kirsten's was sincere, and a decade later we *are* still friends—other than Brad Coleman, whose wedding

I was in Chicago to attend, the oldest friend I have.
For a long time, for no reason other than a sense of
dopey Midwestern boy-meets-girl-next-door destiny,
I expected to eventually marry her. I hadn't thought
of that for a few years. But nine weeks before my
wedding, across town from the apartment tower
where Kirsten now lived, I remembered it as I
walked up the sidestairs of her little brother's dormitory, and it made me laugh.

I went in a side door of
Corcoran Hall as someone was leaving, snuck past the
front desk, and—just before six—woke David up. He
took it pretty well, even though he was hungover, and
we went to the downstairs lobby to catch up on things.

David had been on the golf course the summer
before when I'd suggested the pilgrimage to Elvis's
grave, and he was eager to hear how it had gone.
Though I summarized our visit, I didn't honestly
know how it had gone. Something about that stop felt
incomplete.

David yawned and said he had to study for a
final, and I said I *had* to take a shower. While I went
out to the car and got Bob, David signed us in at the
front desk. We dumped our suitcases in David's room,
and I took a shower that was easily as transcendental
as a full-blown religious conversion. The hot water
kicked me in the head, licked my sides, my butt, my
groin. Tickled my feet. I escaped into—where?—some
other place, stuffed with glitter and magic, chrome
breezes, golden bowties and brass-barreled guns.
Then, on the dorm room's cheap indoor-outdoor car-
peting, I took a long nap and dreamt forgettable
dreams.

For two days we rested. Living and breathing my three ways of looking at tourist traps had become too much work for two lazy Midwestern graduate students. We browsed for hours in first-rate used-book, used-record and used-clothing stores. We ate lunch in quasi-Bohemian cafes whose kitchen help spoke only an animated southern European language that David swore was Serbo-Croat. We played football on the wind-blasted shores of Lake Michigan, giving up when our towels and T-shirts had blown into the lake twice apiece and our eyes were stinging from the sand. Because of the winds, even the zoo was closed. Back at the dorm, for the first time in days, we weren't tourists, and it was an unequivocal relief.

When I was eight Grandpa Bob, my maternal grandfather, taught me about baseball. No one else was going to do it (Dad knows less about sports than I do about intake manifolds), so he bought me a subscription to *The Sporting News* and, when I visited him one summer, took me to my first major league ballgame. That night in St. Louis, Bob Gibson pitched a three-hitter against Houston, and in one inning struck out three Astros on nine straight pitches. Grandpa Bob and I sat behind home plate, listening to Gibson's curveballs slice the heavy riverfront air, and that night a hopeless baseball fan was born.

Bryan, Ohio, is hours from the nearest major league ballpark, but on every family vacation thereafter, I eased that pain by wheedling my parents into stopping for baseball games. Each summer, as we criss-crossed America, I tucked a major league schedule into my underwear drawer on the off-chance that, en route to California, we might pull into Kansas City just as the Royals were taking batting practice. Over the years we went to games in Montreal, Atlanta, Cincinnati, Cleveland, Houston, Arlington, Los Angeles, Seattle and Chicago.

Dad and Shari enjoyed the games as most nonfans do, for the food. Dad drank a lot of beer and Shari ate a lot of ice cream and, by and large, they were happy. They weren't annoyed by artificial turf, they found exploding scoreboards neat instead of vulgar, they didn't keep score and they didn't care who won. But they're family, and I still love them.

Mom was more indulgent. For years she'd put up with Grandpa Bob's incessant baseball talk, and now she had a child who'd picked up where he left off. She humored me, though, listening with feigned interest while I told her about such arcana as Buzz Capra's earned-run average.

Chicago was on our way back to Bryan from just about any point west of the Mississippi, and either the Cubs or the White Sox are always at home, so we stopped there the most—four times in all. The Cubs were Grandpa Bob's favorite team. Not once in his lifetime did they win a World Series, but he never wavered.

While Bob and I were in Chicago, we could have gone to see the White Sox at Comiskey. But I wanted to go instead to a game at the Friendly Confines. So I bought a case of Old Style beer, watched the Cubs on a black-and-white TV in David's room and—at the midpoint of my trip—indulged myself in sentimental thoughts about my heritage.

The night before Brad Coleman's wedding, Bob and I went downtown to meet Kirsten after she got off work and catch the last few minutes of Happy Hour at the Rush Street bars. With David's directions, we rode the El unescorted for the first time in either of our lives.

People were just getting off work, and the sidewalks were a-bustle. In Water Tower Square, at the bottom of the front steps of some historic church, four breakdancers spun and flew to the strained anger of Grandmaster Melle Mel's "White Lines (Don't Do It)" while, a few feet away, a lithe young woman with a violin and a pasty-faced young man with a cello played a pleasant classical something-or-other. The breakdancers' audience, mostly black, and the string duet's audience, mostly white, traded annoyed glares back and forth.

On North Michigan Avenue, a clerk-ish guy about our age, blue blazered and bowtied, had built a small crowd around him. His name was Dan Hurley and, sitting in a director's chair with a wind-up alarm clock at his feet and a battered old Remington manual typewriter on his lap, he was banging out what a sign around his neck billed as 60-SECOND NOVELS. Two young women, giggling and holding each other, were apparently having Hurley churn out their custom-made novel for a fee of five bucks. Bob walked behind Hurley to get a glimpse of the page.

"What's it like?" I whispered.

Bob shrugged. "Silliness, mostly."

"Still," I said, "you'd even have to be a pretty damn good *typist* to churn out a page in sixty seconds."

As it turned out, Hurley spent about three minutes on the "novel." And the two women, once they'd read it, tipped him an extra two dollars.

Hurley used to be an editor for the American

Bar Association and, before going to work every morning, had worked doggedly on his own novel, *Johnny Hero: A Comic Book Tragedy.* When he couldn't get the book published, he hit the streets, hoping to attract attention. The novel still hasn't been published, but what he did attract was money, sometimes as much as $100 a day. He even got written up in *People* magazine, which is where I got all this background stuff, since when he asked us if he could whip us up a masterpiece, we declined and headed down Michigan Avenue.

"That's it," Bob said. "That's how I'll pay for this trip. We'll just set up on a corner in some tourist place—maybe outside Disneyland—and churn these out."

"We don't have a serviceable typewriter."

"We could buy one, and pay it off."

"Too much trouble. Why don't we do it when we get home? We could set up a word processor in a shopping mall, then prey on the housewives and small urchins."

Bob agreed. This would be our path to the Big Money. A much more lucrative part-time job for the young writer than the traditional (and erratic) teaching assistantships, freelance work, bartending and table waiting. As hackwork for quick and tax-free bucks, there's no beating it. Look for us at a mall near you.

"Are you serious?" Kirsten said when we met her after work, heading to the Rush Street bars. "I bet you wouldn't really have the nerve to go through with it."

"It'd be great," I said. "We could—"

"I can't believe you're getting married," she interrupted, gently pinching my arm. "That's—I don't know." She smiled, bright as ice in gin. "That's really terrific. I bet you're excited."

Pushing eleven, after Kirsten gave us a tour of Chicago's finest meat-market bars and we all danced briefly with strangers, Bob and I took the El back to David's.

The first train that roared into the station was packed, so reluctantly we waited for another. The next train was no less full, but we were young, weary and desperate enough to squeeze in. Then, barely underway, still in the underground portion of the route, the train came to a dead halt.

It was no big deal, for a while.

Ten minutes later, when the train had moved no farther than 8 feet, an elderly black man yelled, "Shih! git *along!* I have to take me a dump!"

Everyone laughed, but given the oppressive heat in our car I doubted humors could remain merry for long.

Bob nudged me. "This is awful. This isn't Oxford, Ohio."

"No," I said. "Not at all."

The speaker in our car crackled, and a raspy voice said, "Ladurf ee giraffe, mfurhhh ruff mm ylurrff. Thank you."

"Muh-fuh," the elderly man said. "Speak up, you!"

"We're going to die," Bob said without looking at me.

Neither of us had a watch, but I'm sure we advanced no farther than 100 yards in the next fifteen minutes. In a full and essentially motionless subway car, time coagulates. Maybe the urban veterans of public transportation were capable of handling this, but it was stultifying to a kid from Bryan, Ohio, whose only comparable experience was a year's penance on the schoolbus during the first grade, hunkering down in his seat to avoid the predatory attention of vicious fifth-graders. Not the easiest task, but a lark compared to trying to keep a rein on one's sanity while standing, sweat soaked and half drunk, in the aisle of an El train car that seemed unlikely to budge before the Tricentennial.

"Myrhh shaefer robrummber," the speaker said. "Big curd."

"Train up ahead crashed," said someone standing directly under the speaker. "Gonna be a while. They're still cleaning up the junk."

We heaved a collective moan.

Bob appeared to be asleep on his feet. "That would've been our train," he murmured.

Mentally I began composing a postcard to Laura, then decided to call the minute we got back. If we got back.

After what seemed like a good two hours—though in retrospect I suppose it was no more than thirty minutes—the train abruptly started amidst thunderous applause, reached full speed and then stopped, its whining brakes drowned out by 200 people groaning as one.

"Cruel," Bob said, eyes still closed. "Cruel and unusual. This is *definitely* not Ohio."

The train teased its passengers five more times, then pulled itself aboveground and into the Fullerton platform.

"I think I might kiss the ground," Bob said. "I really do."

David wasn't in his room when we got there, though his roommate said he'd be back any minute. I called Laura collect and, inexplicably, everything was wonderful. Breathless, we talked for ten minutes, never nagging or apologizing, broaching no fractious topics, veering toward an idiosyncratic style of lovesick babytalk and concluding with Laura's insightful appraisal of the new Springsteen record. If I hadn't already proposed to this woman twice before, I'd have done it then, from Chicago to Columbus, over the phone. I hung up, feeling capable of any great task, whatever might come. Karate. Carpentry. Self-knowledge.

We got even drunker and spent the night at the apartment of two punkette classmates of David's. I passed out in an old armchair and, when I woke up, Bob Wakefield was sleeping on the living room couch and Brad Coleman, a friend I couldn't remember not knowing, was about to get married.

I wasn't hungover, but when I stood up my back cracked like a small pack of lady-finger firecrackers. I shook Bob awake and he asked what time the wedding started. "Ten-thirty," I said. "Ten-thirty in the morning. What time is it now?"

"Little after nine."

We hurried back to David's dorm, packed up our stuff and took quick showers.

"The wedding's in Winnetka," I said, tying my tie. "Way, way up on the north side, past Evanston and Skokie and everything."

"You know how to get there?"

"I guess. I have directions. What time's it now?"

Bob moved a pile of clothes away from a clock-radio. "Quarter of ten."

"Oh, Christ." The day before, having discovered that my only jacket was savagely wrinkled from 2,000 miles of jostling in the trunk, I'd dropped it off at some Laotian dry cleaners. "We still have to pick up my jacket. We're going to be late for sure."

Bob shook his head. "This is insane. I've never heard of anyone getting married in the morning."

But by the time we got in the car, Bob had cheered up. "You know, I've never before attended the wedding of someone who broke my nose."

As a Miami University freshman, Brad Coleman, lived down the hall from Bob. One day, while staging a stuntman fistfight on the quad, Brad miscalculated one of his fake blows and sent Bob to the hospital for a full week.

Once in Winnetka, Bob and I slipped into a back pew on what was—I noticed too late—the bride's side. The service was almost over. Even from behind, Brad seemed taller than ever and Margy more lovely. When they turned, Brad's smile was impossibly wide and I saw perfect joy—the kind we'd had as boys, watching well-thrown rotten tomatoes connect with the ass of my neighbor's cat.

The reception was in downtown Chicago at the Urban Men's League, several stories high and filled with scores of paintings and sculptures. My high school chemistry teacher was there, a friend of Brad's family who harbored a grudge because I'd once placed his son in a trash can. He cornered me, explaining the Urban Men's League's now defunct policy for excluding women in the same condescending tone he'd used to explain the proper maintenance of petri dishes. After a long half hour of this, I excused myself and pulled two martinis from the bar.

I had tired of bitching and moaning about food and drinks we couldn't afford. Here, for free, were limitless drinks and a five-course meal. The wedding band was led by a man who had once played with Glenn Miller and, later, the Bozo the Clown studio band. They were corny—as any good wedding band ought to be—but it was the kind of nutty crowd for which a corny wedding band was provocation to be zany. They even played an Elvis medley.

Bob and I danced and danced and danced, mostly with Margy's sisters. Everyone we talked to was entranced by the idea of our trip, charmed by our accounts of Ruby Falls and Elvis's ubiquitous TVs. The people at our table—friends of the bride's parents, none of whom we'd met before—relentlessly fed us with good ideas for other places to visit. "Don't *miss* the Grand Canyon," said a matronly woman. "And Mount Rushmore is *mar*velous. Lyle and I *so* enjoyed the Grand Tetons."

At least ten people told us they wished they could just pick up and go.

As Bob and I left, Brad and Margy Coleman told me that they'd definitely see me in August, at my own wedding.

Only eight blocks away from where we'd parked El Basurero, the Sears Tower was not difficult to find. As we shot skyward in one of the world's fastest elevators, I pretended to be a Latin lounge singer and launched into the Carpenters' second-biggest hit ever: "I yam on top of that worlt . . ." Then I looked around the elevator and realized what a jerk I must've seemed, then decided to forge a brave front.

A gaunt middle-aged man in an Indianapolis Colts cap surveyed me from head to toe. "Are you from England?"

"No."

"California?"

"Ohio."

The man nodded. "Oh, right. On vacation, aren't ya?"

"I guess it shows," I said, resigned.

"We're tourists," Bob chimed. "And you?"

"I'm here on business," the man said. "Meeting tomorrow."

"Too bad," I said, and when the man seemed a bit offended, I added, "Of course, I mean 'too bad' in the best possible way."

He rolled his eyes.

Like most people, we stayed atop the world's tallest structure for hours, doing laps around the observation deck, searching for landmarks, watching the lights of Chicago emerge from the advancing dusk. We each dumped dimes into the telescopes.

A trio of ham radio operators had set up an elaborate rig on the northeast corner of the deck. They explained to us (and another twenty bystanders) that they were playing the ham radio version of hide-and-seek and that somewhere below us, thirty Chicagoans were spending their Saturday seeking the source of their signal. "This is our best one yet," one of the hams said, beaming. "We've got it bouncing off three or four places, including the top of the Hancock building. They'll have to pay to go up there before they'll even *guess* where we are."

"Yeah," said the ham most involved with knob twiddling. "They may not *ever* find us."

The third ham slumped down against the railing of the deck and started in on his sack lunch.

We soon bored of them and headed to the gift-shop, where Bob spotted a day-glo orange bumper sticker. "I visited Sears Tower, Chicago, Illinois: World's Tallest Building"—a must for El Basurero's trunk. "I'll flip you for it," Bob said, producing a coin.

"Heads," I called.

Heads it was, so Bob was stuck with a 79-cent purchase, which, like all the rest, was soon recorded in his little red account book.

"Let's get going," he said. "We've got miles to go before we sleep."

Back at El Basurero, we affixed the bumper sticker to the trunk, a badge of tourism to complement the insect-splattered Ruby Falls placard still clamped to the front bumper. I had to laugh. "Well, whaddaya say? Westward ho or what?"

8
Reconsider Baby

When the groan of an idling Peterbilt woke me, I was still wearing the same clothes I'd danced in at the Urban Men's League. My tie was stuffed in my shirt pocket, though, and my blazer was draped not over a chair back but over me, a poor substitute for a blanket. In the front seat Bob, his head supported by the steering column, rubbed his eyes and whimpered.

"God, I miss David's floor," I said, opening the car door and waiting for enough energy for me to emerge into the morning sunlight of an anonymous rest area. "Is this Iowa? It looks like Iowa. It's Iowa, isn't it?"

"Illinois," Bob said. "Western, I think. I'm pretty sure. I hope. Can you drive?"

I asked for the trunk key, then foraged through my suitcase in search of deodorant, fresh underwear, a semiclean T-shirt and torn, ratty jeans. "Back in a sec," I said, heading to the men's room to change.

The night before Bob had decided that rather than fight traffic, we ought to wait until near midnight to leave town. We wound up back in the Rush Street singles bars—sans Kirsten this time—standing around and, in my case, trying to function despite an abrupt, inexplicable but certain loss of 67 IQ points. Unfortunately I wasn't drunk enough to blame this loss on alcohol. At one point I asked a tall redhead to dance to an undanceable current song. After shucking and weaving my way through it, I asked where she was from.

"Oh, I'm from a little town a half hour from here called Romeoville."

"How far is that from here," I asked.

"About a half hour, like I said."

"Oh yeah, right. Hmm. You know, I've read *Romeo and Juliet.*"

"Well, isn't that nice for us both." She reached under the table for her purse. "Goodbye."

After two hours of that, I bagged it. I found a corner barstool and—looking straight ahead, speaking to no one but the bartender—got stinking drunk.

Bob found me soon after the lights came up for last call. He had a very pretty, very busty brunette in tow. I remember being surprised, since the singles-bar scene is hardly Bob's element. She walked with us to El Basurero, and while I dove into the back to pass out, they kissed and swapped addresses.

Other than a vague sensation of motion and a dim awareness of tires singing and thumping against the worn and periodically pitted interstate, that was my final image of Chicago and the last thing I laid bleary eyes on until that western Illinois rest area.

I stuck my head under the faucet of the men's room's lone sink, clamping my eyelids shut as the cold water shocked my scalp. Then I quickly changed clothes, shook the excess water from my hair and donned a Cincinnati Reds ballcap. I checked the red "You Are Here" dot on the glass-encased roadmap: we were indeed in the western part of the state, about 13 miles from Ohio, Illinois.

"Move over," I said to Bob, still in his defeated, head-against-the-wheel pose. "I'm driving."

"I have to change."

"Well, hurry up. We don't have all day."

Bob Wakefield snickered. "Yes we do. We have all day, and then some."

The Eight Most Unpleasant and Least Topographically Interesting States to Drive Through East to West in One Sitting (Or: These Are Drives That Try Men's Souls):

1. Kansas
2. Nebraska
3. Iowa
4. Oklahoma
5. Pennsylvania
6. North Dakota
7. South Dakota
8. Ohio

As a native of one of those states, I'm acutely aware how condescending the list is. Real life is more complex than passers-through might imagine among these glacially scrubbed plains, often hundreds of miles from the nearest on-ramps. But the dignity and curious interest these states engender are best recorded by sociologists, backroads reactionaries and other people with time on their hands, tenure and grant money in their pockets. That work, once published, may hold great fascination for people with real jobs, Americans whose two weeks of summer vacation don't allow enough time for first-hand observation of noble farmers and above-average children, soybean festivals and hamlets where no one speaks French or pays to park. For those of us on our way to the more immediate pleasures of Disneyland and Universal Studios, the Grand Canyon and the Rocky Mountains, the Midwest is something to be endured, an object lesson in delayed gratification.

What this has created in these states is a parallel-universe community—a ramshackle cement ditch bisecting the state, filled with sleepy truck drivers and out-of-state leadfoots, lined with one hundred gas stations, fireworks sales and fast-food emporia that are repeated in endless, predictable cycles, like the background animation in a low-budget cartoon. The citizens of this long, thin town steer their vehicles with one finger, adjusting for deficiencies in wheel alignment while dreaming of the horizon, passing the time by mentally calculating gas mileage or trying to set a new personal record for miles traveled during the playing time of a Supremes tape. People in the filling stations here have a desperate look in their eyes, born of too many hours with wailing children and the onus of having gotten a late start. The law here brandishes a gun that shoots bullets of radar, and he accepts Visa. No one in this long, thin town has clean hair.

All because this is the second-fastest and by far the cheapest way to get from Point A to Point B.

We were making good time, so we rewarded ourselves.

I drove all the way to Des Moines, where we stopped for gas and lucked into an all-you-can-eat, family-style Sunday buffet at a restaurant featuring Bavarian decor, a waitress with an Australian accent and steaming piles of roast beef and green beans. Bob drove from there to Lincoln, where we stopped to see a movie, choosing the just-released *Ghostbusters*. This was a loud theater, dominated by two rows of teenagers shouting instructions at the screen—"Don't go in *there*—couldn't *pay* me to go in there."—and a few dozen VCR owners too dim to realize they'd left home and come to a large, dark, public room where not everyone needed to be told, "That guy was on 'Saturday Night Live' " or "Here comes the good part." I must confess, however, that Bob and I did do some talking ourselves. At one point in the film, when the titular characters are being celebrated for busting ghosts, they're asked this question by New York talk-show host Joe Franklin: "Well, I guess there's one question all of America wants to know: have you been in contact with Elvis?"

Whereupon Bob and I, in disbelief and unison, said, "Give us this day our daily Elvis," and executed a high-five.

"We almost missed today," I said after the movie, driving toward Colorado and a drab red sunset. "Jeez, that was close, but our record's still perfect."

"I'd have to say it *is* pushing the outer limits of coincidence." Bob rattled through the tape box. "Have you seen Wall of Voodoo?"

The Mileage Chart in our map indicated 1,021 miles between Chicago and Denver, which—by means of comparison—is 113 miles shorter and 114 times less interesting than the drive between Los Angeles and Seattle. Piled on top of the horrible stasis of I-80 through Iowa and Nebraska, eastern Colorado's I-76 seems a cruel joke, particularly the stateline sign: a rough hewn log affair, painted brown, surrounded by sunbaked weeds, distant fencing and powerlines, reading WELCOME TO COLORFUL COLORADO. Sure, pal. You bet, and thank you.

Bob knew the ride well. He'd been here in 1969, when his mother conducted a prototypical post-divorce pile-the-kids-in-the-Pontiac-and-see-America trip. He returned for a few weeks in 1975 to visit his second-eldest sister Joan, who'd moved there. And the summer before he'd worked for a month as a waiter—serving monied vacationers $18 plates of curried elk—in the Black Canyon Lodge, which Joan manages. So, like most travelers who haven't been all that many places, Bob took obvious pleasure in recognizing *everything:* fast-food places where he'd eaten, filling stations where he'd refueled, exits where a member of his family had demanded restroom stops.

By the time we got off I-76, we could see the Rockies, though they were still more than 100 miles away. Through Greeley, then on to Loveland, U.S. 34 ran us through a gauntlet of the New West, which is to say, small towns which feature the juxtaposition of Jeep dealerships and Westernwear outlets with computer supermarkets and Italian bicycle shops—all the while with the Rockies suspended over the hood of El Basurero like a gorgeous threat.

Yet our rusty steed made it huffing and clacking up the 31 miles from Loveland to Estes Park without incident, albeit also without ever reaching 30 miles per hour. The tension that marked previous climbs through the Appalachians was absent this time, ostensibly because we were preoccupied with running out of gas ("There's a gas station right when we get to Estes," Bob said, "I'm pretty sure I've made it with this much gas before"), but more likely because of the prospect of a non-metal roof over our heads and free eats.

We made the Estes Park Texaco just before noon, Mountain Standard Time. Bob told me that the tourist season hadn't started here yet, wouldn't start until after the 4th of July. The main intersection—which has a slot in its traffic-light cycle reserved solely for pedestrians, during which they may walk any whichway, including diagonally—was no more bustling than the intersection of High and Main in Bryan. The Ripley's Believe It Or Not Museum was closed for remodeling.

The Black Canyon Lodge abutted the northern edge of Estes, far enough from touristy downtown and close enough to Rocky Mountain National Park to charge exorbitant rates. Set in a stand of hearty conifers off the main road, the Black Canyon complex included the restaurant, housed in a gable-ceilinged lodge with a mortared-rock porch, and a series of cabins tucked into boulder-strewn recesses in the mountainside. The owners and/or guests must have been persnickety in the extreme, since the first thing Joan did when she saw Bob was tell him to park El Basurero at the bottom of the driveway, out of sight.

When Bob and Joan first saw one another, they neither hugged nor kissed. They spoke as if Bob lived a half hour away and had swung by for a beer, a conversation full of odd, elliptical pauses and sentences completed by committee. After the exchange of how-was-your-trip pleasantries, Bob asked if there was a waiter's job open. Joan wasn't sure.

Bob and I each took a quick shower in Joan's cabin, then went with Joan into town to lunch with the remainder of the Estes Park Wakefield contingent.

I come from a tiny family, the nuclear kind you hear so much about: a mommy and a daddy and a brother and a sister. I have an aunt, an uncle, three cousins and two surviving grandparents. Period. Consequently I have an outsider's interest in the machinations of large families, especially those made yet more scattered, diversified and complex by the lingering effects of divorce. At the end of the summer I would marry into such a family, fraught with divorced and remarried parents, married and unmarried siblings and half-siblings, three sets of grandparents, and a formidable array of aunts, uncles and cousins.

Even though big families capture my imagination, I confess that I have more trouble keeping them straight than I do sorting out the dramatis personae in Russian novels. With the seven Wakefield siblings, this problem is compounded by their soundalike names: Blaine, Bill and Bob; Jane, Joan and Jean. I find it easiest to keep track of the youngest, Polly, if only because of the breach her first name causes in the alliterative gender lines. But on the whole, during their mealtime conversations, I might as well have been watching random episodes of an unfamiliar soap opera.

That first lunch set the tone. In an open-air Estes restaurant, Bob and his three sisters and two of their boyfriends caught up on recent news and put forth the blasé front of the native. I was startled to hear them call my friend "Robby," the only people on the planet to do this. For everyone else, it's "Bob" first and "Robert" second. "Robby," in fact, had never occurred to me.

I was brought into the fold to discuss our trip-to-date (though by now we were already embellishing). But for the most part, I spent lunch gawking at the entertainment—a guitarist who ached to be John Denver—and drinking a yard of ale: a conspicuous 3-foot-high beaker that, when not in use, is supported by a large wooden holder. This contraption makes the consumer look lost and ridiculous, like a Tyrolean shepherd who has wandered into the cafe to sound his horn.

Like Gatlinburg, Estes Park is a National Park fringe town, if a less entrenched one, and it seems to fulfill a roughly approximate function. Though the gourmet taffy shoppes, rubber-reptile boutiques and Believe It Or Not Museum clearly mark Estes as a fringe town, there are touches that one could hardly imagine in a place like Gatlinburg. The fortune teller in the lobby of one of the town's two movie theaters, for example. Or the presence of a pretty good bookstore: dominated, admittedly, by regional histories, guides to indigenous flora and fauna and compendia of gruesome campfire tales, but nevertheless a place where one might buy the collected poems of Yeats or the latest *New Yorker.* Estes Park is, at once, more frontier and more upscale than most fringe towns, though the understandable pull exerted by the majesty of the bordering Rockies makes me suspect that "frontier" and "upscale" are not, in 1984, mutually exclusive. In Estes Park, Colorado, perhaps even in the whole of the much-ballyhooed New West, "frontier" and "upscale" are becoming synonymous.

Since sitting still in Estes Park didn't fulfill my original idea for this trip, I really wanted to get going. After dropping our film off at a one-day photo developer, I gamely spent an afternoon poking through curio shops and a few hours catching lazy hatchery bass in a one-acre pond. Though diverting, this wasn't fishing—not when you rent a rod and pay by the hour. Nor was it sufficiently touristy: tourists should walk away with felt pennants or painted shot glasses, not bloated, squirming smallmouths.

But I understood that Bob wanted to spend some time with his sisters, so I tried not to act restless, even as he cloaked himself in dignity and professed to be embarrassed when I played with various bits of displayed trinketry—embarrassed, he said, because he lived here. Had lived here, anyway. Might live here in the near future.

"I'm out of money," he told me on our way to dinner one night with Polly and her boyfriend Doug.

"All out? Or just really-low out?"

"Out-out. Two dollars and change. My mom was supposed to forward my last assistantship check, but Joan said it hasn't come yet."

"Oh." We wound out of Estes to Polly and Doug's in silence, save for the transmission straining to make it halfway up Giant Track Mountain. I knew that if a cushy waiter's job opened up, Bob might well abandon me. But Joan had told him not to count on anything, and I figured the trip was a lock. Now, for the first time, I realized that Bob might well stay in Estes, job or no.

The meal was really more of a party—a festive and convenient excuse for Bob and I not to talk to each other for several hours.

Afterward we sat on the hood of El Basurero, 6,500 feet above sea level, and looked across a skyful of moonlit snowcaps. Without looking at me, Bob outlined contingency plans. He said he'd drive me to the nearest airport and I could fly home. Or, he said, he had this friend in Denver—a guy I'd never met—who might want to take a trip. Or maybe once the tourist season got underway, we both could find jobs in Estes. Or maybe I could even take his car, though he said he'd have to mull that one over.

Polly and Doug let us stay at their place that night. Bob and I flipped for the sofabed, and I lost.

In the morning we climbed Giant Track Mountain. With tennis shoes and no climbing experience, we had little hope of reaching the 9,300-foot summit. But it was a perfect morning—even though we got temporarily stranded on the sheer face of a cliff, learning the hard way that it's easier to climb up than down—that gave us a chance to work off a little aggression, and to think.

I sat with my feet dangling off a cliff, trying to decide what Bob would do. A hawk flew past, no more than 10 feet from my face. I'd have made a pathetic Indian, I thought, having no idea what to make of this particular omen.

When we finally made it down, the tension between us had entirely eased. We agreed to go into town to pick up our photos and have a few beers, and that's when we first saw the Miracle Photo.

The rest of the photos were pleasant, if ordinary: shots of the Ruby Falls trash can, a Memphis shop window full of black mannequin heads, our new haircuts in Chicago; driving pictures featuring drivers unkempt, unshaven and resolute; amateurish attempts at picture-postcards. As a whole, they were conclusive proof that the camera worked fine, but the flash was finished.

And the Miracle Photo? Well, this was a shot of the Pigeon Forge Elvis Presley Heartbreak Motel. Over the Elvis Presley Boulevard sign, there was a double exposure of three nuns, one of whom brandished what appeared to be a set of hedge clippers.

"Did you take any pictures of nuns," I asked.

Bob shook his head. "No. And I'm sure I didn't photograph any hedge clippers."

I didn't know whether to laugh or be amazed. The Miracle Photo, I decided, was conclusive proof that there's something to this Elvis thing.

I watched Bob study the nuns, and resisted the temptation to offer him money for his analysis.

9

Good Rockin' Tonight

We left Estes Park on June 13. I'd enjoyed my time with Bob's family; they fed and housed us well. But as we rode El Basurero out of Estes through Roosevelt National Forest on tortuous U.S. 36—a road Polly claims to have driven at 65, which is either a hell of an exaggeration or proof of psychosis—I was never so happy to leave a place.

This was the linchpin of the trip.

Until this drive *out* of Estes—momentous otherwise only for the not unlikely possibility that automotive trouble would mean a fatal plummet off a Rocky—it was possible that the trip would end *in* Estes. In my gut I was pretty sure Bob would feel too bad about aborting the trip to stay here and look for work, but he kept me guessing about his level of commitment until the day we actually left. Throughout our layover, Bob prefaced all future trip plans with "if," never "when." As in, "If we go to Disneyland . . ."

So we waited for Bob's check to arrive, and he reminded me, ever so matter-of-factly, that since I'd cost him a job, several hundred dollars and maybe the final bit of life in his 1967 Chevrolet, I'd have no recourse to indignation should he ask me to grab the next interstate back to Ohio. At the time I was too obsessed with worry to remember that at no time had I held a gun to his head and forced him to accompany me across America. In fact, he made me feel as if I had, back in Oxford, even cocked the hammer.

So we discussed alternatives. The one Bob mentioned most was lending me El Basurero, either to drive the rest of the way or to go back to Oxford. "Whatever you want to do," he said with a shrug—a shrug, I'd bet, that masked a gleeful image of me stranded on a stretch of desolate Kansas interstate, an automotive ignoramus, easy prey for any unscrupulous jayhawk mechanic who hoped for one big score that would allow him to pay off his satellite dish. Don't ask me how: I know that's what Bob was thinking. Granted, his offer was prompted partly by guilt and partly by altruism, but vengeance had to figure in there somehow.

After a few days, however, when it was obvious that Joan couldn't deliver a job, Bob asked Jean for $200. He promised to stop in Estes Park on our way back to Ohio—"in July, I guess"—and sign the assistantship check over to her, thus providing her with about $30 in interest. She wrote him a check and we cashed it on our way out of town, minutes before the bank closed.

By the time we left the city limits, we were equally committed to the rest of the trip—especially because the next free place to stay, our next real stop, was my grandmother's apartment in Tucson, Arizona, 959 miles away.

I was six years old. I had a pineapple haircut. It was 1968.

My family was taking a vacation through the

Rocky Mountains, towing a 27-foot Wilderness travel-trailer with a canary-yellow Buick Electra, touring national parks, ghost towns and at least fifteen sites of famous gunfights bordered by cemeteries named Boot Hill.

Colorado was fruitful stomping ground for all of the above. My memories of the trip are fragmented, though I vividly remember three things: a cowboy giftshop in Montana that sold cap rifles and plastic chaps; a desire in Yellowstone to throw two-year-old Shari into a scalding mudpot; and Mom saying repeatedly, "I could live here, I really could. This is *so* beautiful." I'd like to say I remember what happened in Central City, Colorado, but I don't. Sometimes I think I do, just as sometimes I think I remember biting Grandpa Bob's nose the day I was brought home from the hospital. In both cases, of course, it's because the story long ago joined the ranks of our family's one-hundred-and-twice-told-tales.

Anyway, we'd been poking around all day in Black Hawk, Idaho Springs and Central City, three "ghost" towns west of Denver, not far off I-70. Like most ghost towns near the interstate, these require quotation marks around "ghost" because several hundred people live there to live off tourists. We arrived at Central City last, parking on the outskirts of town in a lot adjacent to an abandoned gold mine. It was dark by the time we finished seeing the sights, and either Mom or Dad (they still argue about this) suggested we spend the night in the parking lot. Outside the abandoned Glory Hole Mine. The moon was full.

Mom took Shari and me inside while Dad uncoupled the car and cranked the tongue-jack so that the weight of the trailer wouldn't rest all night on the hitch. Later Dad said he thought he heard crying, and he assumed it was Shari. But Shari had *not* been crying.

About 3 A.M. Mom and Dad were awakened by the faraway sobbing of a child. "You could tell, from the way it sounded, that he was running and crying," Mom says. "You know how that sounds, when a little kid is running and crying." She sat up and saw a bright light shining through the rear window of the travel-trailer, the window facing the mine.

"Markie?" Shari said, now awake, thinking I was the problem. "Markie?" I was, and would continue to be, deep in sleep.

Mom made Dad get up and look out the windows. "We were spooked," she says. "I mean *spooked.*"

Then the light vanished, the crying ceased and they went back to sleep.

About an hour later, a Jeep began doing laps around our rig, driving as close and as fast as possible without hitting either the Buick or the Wilderness. Mom and Dad were afraid to sit up and get a better look. No human noises issued from the Jeep, no drunken whoops, no boisterous laughter, no sobs. "We thought it would go on forever," Mom says. "That was the last trip your Dad took without a gun." Finally, after "a good fifteen minutes," the Jeep drove off.

At dawn Mom and Dad leapt from bed, woke their children and began hasty preparations to leave. I helped Dad hook the trailer back up to the car. In the dust there were Jeep tracks circling our rig, but none coming or going. I asked Dad about it. "Your mother will tell you," he said, "after we get the show on the road."

Which we did, and she did. I thought it was a good scary story. I don't remember if I believed it.

Mom's a sane, stable sort, though, so I suppose I did. And despite the story's implausibility, I suppose I believe it still.

Which is more than Mom herself did after a couple days. Some kids' prank, she began to think. Or maybe we imagined it, being so tired and all.

So why did Shari wake up?

It *really* sounded like a crying child, right?

Why didn't the Jeep tracks lead back to the road?

My mother has never purchased a copy of the *National Enquirer,* and she's hardly the type to concoct a story for it. There must be *some* explanation, she reasoned, which gave her an excuse to assimilate and thereby forget that night outside Central City.

Until, in a Golden, Colorado, bookstore a few days hence, she purchased a book on local ghost towns. She read it to us in the car as we headed through Kansas on I-70. And one chapter was called "The Legend of the Glory Hole Mine."

After the gold trailed out in the Glory Hole Mine, people began to move away from Central City. The mine eventually closed, but was poorly sealed off. Children, simultaneously so enamored of and oblivious to danger, played on the trailings around the mine shafts and, inevitably, one day a six-year-old boy fell in. Rather than staying put while his friends went for help—as any television-era child reared on the sagas of Timmy and Lassie would know to do—he panicked and ran. And ran and ran and ran. The rescue party arrived bearing lanterns and searched for days in the dark mine. They could hear him through the walls, but he was bawling too hard to hear their pleas to be quiet and stay in one place. By the time they found him, he was dead.

And legend has it that on some nights, especially under a full moon, you can see the searchlights and hear the boy crying as he runs toward his death in the Glory Hole Mine.

"**W**hat about the Jeep," Bob asked when I told him the story. "What does that have to do with the dead kid?" He pulled El Basurero into a Central City parking lot on the opposite end of town from the Glory Hole Mine.

I shrugged. "Beats me. The way I look at it, it makes the whole story more believable. Honest-to-God visits from the supernatural can't be explained away so perfectly."

Bob said nothing, but his mood brightened. We'd taken an unnecessarily scenic route there, coming in the back way on Colorado 7 rather than the slightly longer but considerably flatter I-25 and I-70. We saw a lot of great stuff: a few hundred mountains, a half dozen elk and a *Rocky Mountain News* vending machine alongside a stretch of road that must've been five miles from the nearest dwelling. All of which would've been less harrowing had we been piloting a more reliable automobile. But with El Basurero death lurked on every corner. For a half hour Bob had been squinting and biting the hell out of his lower lip. I could tell he already regretted his decision to leave Estes Park or, at the very least, his acquiescence when I'd suggested a visit to Central City. "It'll be great," I said. "We have to go to at least one fake ghost town. It's our duty as Ohioans." I waited until we were driving through Black Hawk to tell him the Glory Hole Mine story, which of course was the real reason for our detour.

We got out of the car and headed down the main drag past the once abandoned, now restored opera house, without which no nineteenth-century boomtown is deemed complete. "You know," I said, "we could sleep here. Instead of driving through all night, I mean."

"No," Bob said without looking up.

Did I really want to sleep there? Would an atheist buy a ticket to see Christ rise from the dead?

It was not yet dark. A handful of tourists walked the streets of Central City, most of them heading the other way, toward their cars and campers in the parking lots. The giftshops and Gay Nineties ice cream parlors were closing down. Bob and I browsed through an antique store that seemed to specialize in rusted license plates, chromatic postcards and Coke bottles from the '20s. I asked the man at the cash register what time it was.

"Seven. Seven sharp."

"Pretty early for all the shops to close, isn't it?" I said.

The man rubbed his hands on the old-fashioned shopkeeper's apron he wore, then shrugged. "Not especially. Still cold up here, up in the high country. Tourist season doesn't begin until, oh, about next week or so." He removed his round wire-rims, blew hot breath on them, and began to polish them on the apron. "Next week everybody'll be open until nine, ten. Thereabouts. You know, tourist season."

He reminded me of the retired postman in the Gatlinburg wax museum—bored, waiting blankly for the first day of the annual onslaught. I sifted through a shoebox of sixty-year-old postcards. "Tourist season," I chuckled to myself. Funny term, now that I thought about it. Makes tourists sound like trout or grapes, like a cash crop to be harvested. Which is, of course, exactly how this man would see it.

A family—a Mom, a Dad and three little girls— entered the store with a formidable ruckus. I'd become mildly engrossed by a postcard depicting a red Packard alongside Route 66 in Vega, Texas, and I ignored them at first. The Mom and the Dad were telling some animated story to the shopkeeper, and finally their waving arms and breathlessness made me look up.

"As big as this, I swear to God." The Mom—who

looked remarkably like mine—made a tomato-sized circle with her hands.

The man behind the counter shook his head. "Never can tell about mountain weather."

"You didn't get any of it," the Dad asked.

The shopkeeper shook his head.

"Not a bit?"

"Nope. Rained about two minutes, then it stopped."

"Take a look," the Mom said. "I mean, will you look at that?" She was pointing out the front window. "For the love of Pete."

The shopkeeper walked to the window. "I'll be," he said, and then walked back behind the counter.

I saw Bob standing by the door, laughing silently. He caught my eye and motioned me over.

The station wagon in front of the store was pitted all over, covered with thousands of melting BB-sized hailstones. On our way in we'd encountered neither rain nor hail.

"Pretty strange," Bob said.

"This will cost a *fortune* to fix," said the Mom, near tears. "My God. A *fortune.*"

"We have insurance, Susan," said the Dad. "After all."

Looking at them, I felt more fortunate. At the time I figured it was the relief we feel at the misfortunes of others: *Thank God it didn't happen to us.* But in retrospect I realize that the hailstones would've added character to El Basurero's looks, and that I felt more fortunate because *my* family's Central City ordeal made for a better story.

We poked around a little while longer amongst the restored facades of Central City. Most everything was closed. We looked in the windows and walked into the lobby of a wax museum, where Bob ordered an ice cream in a huge sugar waffle and I examined a cigar-store cowpoke who talked out of a speaker concealed under his buckskin shirt. I told him that sixteen years back my parents had taken a photo of me sitting in his lap. Then Bob and I strolled to the south edge of town, to the parking lot outside the Glory Hole Mine. "A fine place to sleep," I said, "don't you think?"

"Either way, you're going to be disappointed," Bob answered, slurping at the ice cream oozing through the soggy cone. "Either nothing would happen, which would be bad, or something would happen, which would be worse."

"Yeah. Whatever. We'll see."

We headed back to El Basurero.

A wooden sign on the sidewalk in front of the Silver Dollar Saloon read:

> FULL MOON NIGHT!
> 16 oz. Coor's drafts
> ONLY 75 CENTS!
> Dusk-Midnight

"I'm not quite ready to face driving down these mountain roads," Bob said. "Let's have a beer."

Bob didn't really like beer, and his near abstinence made my moderate quaffing feel like the early stages of alcoholism. Which it might be, but I was, of course, happy to oblige.

We sat at the bar. Like everywhere else in Central City, the Gilded Garter Saloon was more or less empty. Three women and a fat guy in a filling-station uniform were clustered around a pinball machine, and a bearded man in a Stetson was talking to the tall, balding, red-vested bartender. We ordered two frosty mugs of Coors and I went to the bathroom.

When I got back, Bob was sweeping his eyes over the room as if it were a museum exhibit. "This is the first bar I was ever in. In 1968."

"No way. *I* was here in 1968. Well, I mean, not

here, but in Central City. When were you here, what month?"

"August."

"*I* was here in August. We could've sat right across the room from each other."

The bartender asked if we needed another, and we said yes. "Call me Rabbit, gents," the bartender said. "Everyone calls me Rabbit."

Actually, we hadn't called him anything, but we nodded. Rabbit it was.

"Fantastic deal, isn't it? The beer, I mean." Rabbit spoke with the kind of stagey, authoritative voice most commonly found emanating from rural radio stations' drive-time deejays.

Rabbit turned the bar's stereo from the Denver station that had been playing to the tape he'd just put in, the soundtrack from *The Big Chill.* "Great fucking movie," he said, looking at us, the kind of statement that demands a reply.

"Yeah, I liked it," I said. "I have a friend, though, who's the same age as the people in that movie, and he *hated* it. He said he didn't know any of those people, I guess because they were all so rich and stuff, and he said he thought *Return of the Secaucus Seven* kicked *The Big Chill*'s butt."

"Hey," Rabbit said. "They're both great movies. *I'm* that age, though. And I knew those people. Plus," he jabbed a thumb toward the stereo, "*The Big Chill* had this music. Man, I felt like I was watching the soundtrack of my own life, do you know what I mean?"

Rabbit asked us what had brought us to Central City. Initially Bob tried to pretend he was a native, as he had in Estes Park, but after a while he backed off and we gave the bartender a synopsis of our trip.

Rabbit pointed at his chest with both thumbs. "I've been traveling more or less straight through since I dropped out of school. 1971." He smiled like a game-show host. "When you're a bartender, you can go anywhere. You have a marketable skill, and you can walk into any good bar in America, and you'll by God have yourself a job for the asking."

"I was a bartender," I said. "Last summer."

"Like it?"

"Not bad," I shrugged. "Not good. But not bad."

"But see," Rabbit said. "So long as you can give the phone number of the owner of that bar and that person'll give you a good recommendation, shoot, you can find work without even half trying, anywhere in the U.S. of A. I ought to know. That's what I do." He slapped himself on the butt. "I keep a list of my former employers in my wallet at all times. All times. I got a good twenty numbers in here, big bars, little bars, in-between bars. Every place from Jersey to Frisco. I haven't been in one place longer than six months for forever."

He saw our beers were nearly gone and wiggled his eyebrows mugward. We nodded, then downed the dregs while he filled two more frosty mugs.

"There you go, gents. Yeah, I just came here from Reno. I had to get out of *that* place, let me tell you. Easy money, easy money, easy money. Let me tell you: it fucks with people's values. Blows them out of the water. People get crazy and forget, when they're at the table or in front of those damn machines, man, they forget where the money that they're dumping down came from. Sad. I'm not kidding. You don't see it so much when you visit, but workin' there, I was all the time seein' otherwise fine folks cryin' in a corner cause they blew their kid's college fund at the fuckin' blackjack table. And winning: that's worse. People do the impossible and beat the fuckin' odds, and then they run all around town buying drinks for strangers and lighting cigars with fifty-dollar bills."

He stepped away to wait on the Stetsoned guy

at the end of the bar. On the stereo, Marvin Gaye sang "I Heard It Through the Grapevine," and Rabbit sang along. "Marvin!" he shouted at the instrumental break. *"Whoo!* We miss you, Marvin."

"You fellas into trivia," Rabbit asked when he came back.

"I've never lost a game of Trivial Pursuit," Bob said. "No one's ever come close."

I'd humbled him once in the All-Star Sports edition, but he was otherwise undefeated and I chose not to quibble.

Rabbit fancied himself a trivia fiend. He had a stack of trivia books under the bar, and an encyclopedic knowledge of the '60s, which he called "my damn era." We jousted with him admirably. Bob was as impressed by Rabbit's grasp of international seats of government as I was by his *Wizard of Oz* minutiae. Bob and I faltered badly only on a gauntlet of James Bond questions. And once we were on sports, I had them both nailed.

"Okay, everybody knows Jackie Robinson was the first black man to play in the majors, right, and that Frank Robinson was the first black to manage in the majors. Okay. So this is a two-parter. (A) Who was the second black player and (B) who was the second black manager?"

Bob soon gave up, but for five minutes Rabbit paced back and forth behind the bar with his hand over his eyes, murmuring "Oh shit."

We ordered another round.

Rabbit delivered them, then leapt in the air. "A-*ha.* Gotcha. The second player was Larry Doby, Cleveland Indians. My team. Good ballplayer."

"What about the manager?"

"Oh shit."

Rabbit made me swear not to tell him. Bob decided cigars were now in order, and left in search of stogies. Rabbit changed the tape to an Elvis Presley greatest hits set.

Give us this day our daily Elvis, I thought.

Rabbit served beers to the quartet at the pinball machine, then came back. "I know I'm gonna know it when you tell me," he said. "But go ahead."

"Also Larry Doby. Also the Cleveland Indians."

"Well, I'll be damned. I'll be dipped in shit." Rabbit poured himself a draft, his first. "I mean, that's my old stomping grounds. Where in Ohio did you say you were from?"

"I'm from northwest. Bob's from central. We went to school at Miami."

Rabbit laughed. "Redskins, eh? I was engaged to this girl who went there. Pretty. Her granddad owned something like fifteen TV stations. I screwed up. One of those long-distance things that never work out. I was going to Youngstown State at the time."

Rabbit began to wax poetic about Youngstown while, inexplicably, he juggled three limes. In the background Elvis sang "In the Ghetto." By the time Bob handed me a stubby black cigar, Rabbit was talking about his time at Kent State—"As fucking fate would have it, the semester of the shootings."

The limes rotated smoothly, flawlessly. Elvis sang "Kentucky Rain."

Rabbit hadn't even been on campus that day. He heard about it on the news, "like everybody else." A woman he carpooled with called him and said, "Did you hear the good news? Classes are cancelled tomorrow." "Can you believe that shit?" Rabbit said. "I hung up and the next day, three credits short of my B.A., I dropped out of school and left home and I haven't been back ever since."

A pretty impressive gesture, I thought.

Bob began writing a letter to a mutual friend of ours on the cardboard bar coasters. He filled up the fronts and then had me fill up the backs. I'd drunk a few more than he had, and my penmanship proved predictably large and erratic. I remember trying to explain in the letter our bizarre string of daily encounters with Elvis.

Outside it was dark. The full moon was obscured by cloud cover and then it began to rain.

Without asking, Rabbit picked up my mug and filled it. Bob looked and me and shook his head. *Not another,* he was thinking. *Now I'll have to drive all night.*

"On the house," Rabbit said. "For Larry Doby." He slapped me on the shoulder. "And for being a fellow bartender. You know: professional courtesy. Like how cops don't give speeding tickets to other cops."

"Thanks," I said. "Thanks a lot."

"Yep," Rabbit said. "I haven't been back to Youngstown since." He reached under his vest and pulled out a large square envelope. An invitation. "My folks forwarded this, just got it today. Invitation to my high-school class reunion. Twenty fucking years. Can you believe that?"

"We both graduated in '79," Bob said. "So our high schools are having five-year reunions this summer. Five years seems hard for me to believe, but twenty, that must be something."

"Fuckin' A, that's something. You guys going?"

"No," I said. "I'm supposed to get married that day."

"Congrats, man." He poured me another free beer, placing it beside the half-empty one in front of me. "That's something I've never had the balls to do."

I thanked him.

"Yeah. Well, anyhow, for my class reunion, I'm gonna rent a big black Cadillac and a couple of the best babes money can buy." He ran his hands over the top of his head. "See, I had all my hair in high school, and so now I look a whole lot different, obviously. I'm gonna rent the most expensive tux in the world, too. And then I'm gonna go in there, refuse to fill out one of those nametags, and make the sonsabitches *guess* who I am." I jumped as Rabbit slammed his fist down on the bar and guffawed. "That's style," he said.

Bob said he'd have to consider that for his own reunion.

We finished our four bar-coaster letter, snuffed our cigars and headed out. "I'll see you guys another time," Rabbit called to us. "If not here, then in some other bar, some other place, some other time." He pointed a finger at us like a gun and made a "pow" noise. "Count on it."

The streets of Central City were wet, but the rain had stopped. "Of all the people I've ever met," Bob said, and then he paused.

"He was one of them."

"Right."

Mentally I formulated a final, feeble plea to spend the night outside the Glory Hole Mine. I never said a word. We got in El Basurero and headed through the night toward Denver.

"Wake up," Bob said. "I have a great idea. It's something we have to do. We just have to. It's out of our hands. This is perfect."

When I'd fallen asleep, we'd been on I-70, heading toward I-25 South and, presumably, the wilds of New Mexico. I rubbed my eyes, tossed my pillow in the backseat and tried to figure out where we were. It wasn't an interstate, and it certainly wasn't New Mexico. There were stoplights and truckstops. "Where are we," I said, "Denver?"

"Yes." He pulled into a Mister Donut parking lot. "We're going to see Ed Sullivan."

Bob got out of the car and went to a pay phone. Ed Sullivan? Oh yeah. Not *the* Ed Sullivan, but some friend of Bob's who'd transferred from Miami to Montana State, I forget why. To major in forestry, maybe. Come to think of it, Bob had mentioned that he was living in Denver and that we ought to visit him. This was in Nebraska, I think, but I'd forgotten all about it. No, he mentioned it in Estes. Ed Sullivan was the guy Bob said might want to take the rest of the trip with me. I went into Mister Donut and ordered a creampuff.

Bob came in and ordered a medium coffee—45 cents, which he noted in that damned expense ledger.

"What's the scoop?"

"He has both. Bananas. Peanut Butter. Both."

"Elvis sandwiches. In Denver. Perfect."

Ed Sullivan lived in a townhouse on the north edge of Denver, requiring a bit of backtracking on I-25 and some meandering among suburban cul-de-sacs. It was 2 A.M. when we arrived. Bob hadn't seen Ed Sullivan in two years, and I'd never met him. He looked sleepy.

As they exchanged information on mutual acquaintances, I fought sleep and was functionally unsociable.

After a while Ed produced two bananas, a butter knife, a loaf of white bread and a jar of Peter Pan. Bob explained why we wanted to eat this particular snack at this particular location. Ed nodded and apparently didn't find it especially strange that a stranger and an old friend would stop by in the middle of the night for peanut-butter-and-banana sandwiches.

We touched the sandwiches together as if they were beer steins, our toast to Elvis Presley.

10

Spinout

Soon after dawn, near Miami, New Mexico, I woke up with a mild hangover, a woolen tongue, and the disharmonious taste of beer and bananas. I was sprawled across El Basurero's backseat without any memory of getting there. "How you doing," I asked Bob. "You tired or anything? Do you want me to drive?"

Through his sunglasses, Bob stared straight ahead, southward down I-25, where only the curvature of the earth obstructed the view to Mexico, 300 miles away. "You've been asleep forever."

"Is that a yes?" On the right side of the road was the snow-capped Sangre de Christo Range of the Rocky Mountains. There wasn't a vehicle in sight—"sight" in this part of America being the rough equivalent of Delaware.

"I'm fine." He placed his 3-D glasses—left over from the American pavilion at the World's Fair—over the sunglasses, then removed the leather necktie hanging from the rearview mirror and began to chew it.

"I'll drive. Why don't you let me drive?"

Bob placed a dirty T-shirt on his head and attempted to fashion it into a babushka. "I'm not tired, but if you want to drive, you can drive. We'll need gas before too awful long." He pulled El Basurero to the shoulder, changed places with me and—for the first time—fell asleep while I drove.

Its perfect, relentless surface notwithstanding, this interstate was a harrowing road, almost devoid of exits, flanked by desolate ranchland, the Rocky Mountains and the Santa Fe Railroad—which, that morning, carried by far the longest freight train I had ever seen. Even as the day emerged, packs of cars and trucks did not. I saw fellow humans approximately every five minutes, and then only for an instant. Bob muttered in his sleep as I pushed his poor, aged automobile near 80.

As we came over one of the few rises in the road, on the shoulder stood a middle-aged man, holding the hand of a little girl with his left hand, thumbing for a ride with his right. We shot by, my reactions dulled by the after effects of Full Moon Night. A quarter mile past them I lifted my foot from the gas, intending, for a moment, to stop. But then I glanced around El Basurero; with all the dirty clothes, newspapers, souvenirs and food wrappers, there hardly seemed room for two passengers. I re-accelerated. Besides, I thought, what sort of guy would be out hitchhiking with his daughter in this part of the country? Maybe, following a futile custody battle, he kidnapped the child from her mother and lit out for Mexico. Or maybe this wasn't the father at all.

By this time we were five miles past them, and all I could think of was a recent widower, down on his luck, desperate for work, thumbing his way across New Mexico with his beautiful, hungry daughter as the sun rose ever higher in the sky.

For the next hour I daydreamed about the man and the child—often considering doubling back for them—as I punished the accelerator for my lack of compassion.

Just past Las Vegas, New Mexico, Bob awoke abruptly. "Gas."

"What?"

"We need gas."

I looked at the gauge, for the first time since I'd begun driving. "We still have an eighth of a tank."

"No way," he scoffed, leaning over to prove me wrong.

"Okay, maybe closer to a sixteenth. I can see blue between the needle and 'empty.'"

"Why'd you pass that exit back there?"

"I don't know. Wasn't paying attention. This is a damn boring road."

Bob opened the map to New Mexico, whispering snippets of mileage figures to himself. "We can make it to Santa Fe," he concluded. "If you can drive a steady speed, there's no reason we can't make it that far. And anyway, if there are any gas stations next to some of these crossroads-exit deals, I'm pretty sure they'd be unbelievably expensive."

"I'm not walking."

"You won't have to. We'll make it." Bob rummaged around in the backseat until he found what he wanted: a small bag of hardened circus peanuts. He crammed four in his mouth at once, grimacing, exacting masochistic pleasure from each bite. "God, these are terrible," he said, reaching in the bag for more. "We'll make it, as long as you keep your speed steady."

I slowed to 55 and tried to keep my foot steady on the gas pedal. I kept my eye on the gauge, willing the needle to stay still. We passed a few exits, though I would've abandoned the Santa Fe edict for an early fill-up if I'd seen a gas station at any of them.

As we neared Santa Fe, Bob busied himself with intense scrutiny of the map and some quick scribbling on the bag from the Sears Tower Giftshop. I turned on the radio. The end-of-the-news item on an Albuquerque AM station concerned the several thousand dollars paid at a Chicago auction yesterday for a limousine. There was a brief, breathless interview with the buyer, a rich young man audibly thrilled to own a vehicle that had once belonged to none other than Elvis Presley.

"Give us this day our daily Elvis," I said with reverence. "Do you think there's any other dead person you could encounter in some way, every day, all across the U.S.A.? I doubt it."

"That's an Albuquerque station, right? Okay." Bob tapped his finger on the map. "I was trying to figure if we can make it to Albuquerque. I think we can, but that—that's proof."

"It's completely on E," I countered, passing the first three Santa Fe exits.

"One time I made it from Oxford to Cincinnati and back with it on E. It's sixty miles to Albuquerque. We can make that."

"This is crazy." But I really loved the idea, despite—or perhaps *because*—of the possibility that we might become stranded in the desert, forced to walk 20 miles at midday. For 60 miles we would be pioneers, adventurers. We would elevate mere interstate-highway driving to a manly test of survival. I slowed El Basurero to 50 and didn't even consider the next two off-ramps.

Halfway to Albuquerque, it didn't look like we'd make it. We rolled up all the windows and held our breath, until sweat soaked through our clothes.

"If we make it," Bob said between gasps of breath, "what we'll do is roll down the windows and drink a beer, just as we coast into the gas station."

I slowed to 40. The needle was well to the left of E.

On the Albuquerque corporate limits, El Basurero coughed and sputtered. Each of us drew in a new lungful of air, then the car discovered a tiny reserve of new life, managing just enough forward propulsion to roll most of the way into a Shell station. When it came to a stop, we each exhaled, frantically rolled down our window, drained a Schlitz and laughed: crazed gringo turistas delivered safely from the desert.

We kept laughing as we pushed the car the final 30 feet to the pumps.

Truth or Consequences lies at the southern end of Elephant Butte Reservoir—created by a damn in the Rio Grande—in southwestern New Mexico, not very far from the covert munitions atrocities going on at White Sands Missile Range. It is, to the best of my knowledge, the only American community named for a game show. The town was known as Hot Springs until, in 1950, Ralph Edwards brought his shenanigan-chocked laugh-riot radio show here for a publicity stunt, for which the grateful city changed its name. This event is still celebrated with an annual fiesta, over which Ralph Edwards still presides. The town doesn't offer much besides gas stations and motels, but of these there are scores—probably near the world's per-capita record—owing to Truth or Consequences's prime location in the very nexus of nowhere.

From the gas station I called my grandmother in Tucson, warning her we'd be arriving late that night. This would've been an uneventful pitstop except that, on the way out of town, a five-iron from I-25, there came a crescendo of hissing and a tiny, sickening explosion as El Basurero's radiator spewed steam and scalding droplets of spent antifreeze.

In the passenger seat, I recited a succinct litany of profanity. Bob, of course, reacted hardly at all. Eschewing speech and visible emotion, he pulled over, turned off the car, opened the hood and walked briskly back toward town. He returned with two gallons of coolant.

I got out to look under the hood and offer my help. I realized I didn't *know* what to do, but was hoping Bob would break his silence long enough to assign a menial task.

He expelled a short, disdainful and exasperated snicker. "Well, this might be the end. If it's a boilover, fine. But if the radiator's cracked—"

I didn't want him to finish that sentence. "So, how much was the antifreeze?"

"Seven-ninety," he muttered.

"Is that high? That's probably high, right?"

"Two bucks at K-Mart."

"Oh."

For an hour we hardly spoke. Bob manipulated caps and hoses and belts and other automotive miscellany I don't understand, often jerking his hand back after touching something unexpectedly hot. At first I hovered, eager at least to watch, frightened and guilty that this might be the end of the car, the end of the trip, maybe the end of the friendship. Twice, Bob sent me back to the Amoco for more precious Prestone. I'd have been relieved if he'd lit into me with elaborate, decimating epithets, even if he'd shoved or slapped me around a little. But calm and quiet, he only shook his head in disgust.

After two sorry attempts, Bob managed to coax the engine to life.

"Is it going to be all right," I asked.

He put the car in gear, drove back into Truth or

Consequences and parked under the carport of a boarded-up motel.

"Well?" I said.

"I don't know, *Mark.*" He gathered up the empty coolant containers, filled them with water at a nearby Texaco and returned to drench the still hot motor. "Probably not."

But when after two hours we finally paroled ourselves from the sweltering roadside of Truth or Consequences, El Basurero seemed adequately revived. Granted, Bob didn't venture above 45 and stopped at every exit and rest area to allow the beast a meager rest in whatever shade was available.

Instead of taking north-south I-25 all the way to the junction of east-west I-10 in Las Cruces, we picked up New Mexico 26 at Hatch, a detour chosen (1) to give El Basurero a break from interstate highways, (2) to sample a token rural road and (3) to save 49 miles. Our map showed the area to be a conspicuous absence: no little triangles designating mountains; no patch of green dots indicating a national park, forest or monument; no pink stripes warning of army bases; and certainly no circles for towns.

New Mexico 26 was beyond smooth—even more perfect than the New Mexican interstates, which is to say it looked as if it had been buffed by hand with a shoebrush. On this kind of road, it's almost safe to drive 100, and judging from the five ranch-pickups we encountered, we were the only motorists in northeast Luna County not afraid of that "almost."

Our only stop was in Nutt. Not on our map and surely unincorporated, Nutt, New Mexico, amounted to the Nutt Cafe and Bar, the Nutt General Store, a house trailer behind the store and a parking lot of rocks, sand, woody plants and rusty pieces of fencing. The two establishments were painted the dullest possible shade of gold. The store was no bigger than El Basurero and was closed for the day. A pre-fab shoe-box, the cafe/bar had a TV antenna on its roof, a Falstaff beer sign out front and, painted above the door, the greeting WELCOME TO THE MIDDLE OF NO-WHERE.

Bob parked in front beside a Ford Torino and a Chevy pickup, each of which were bronze and white roofed. He checked the radiator and, after deeming it to be properly radiating, said he wanted ice cream. "Vanilla. Or maybe a Buster Bar. The owner's probably around somewhere." He set off for the trailer.

I went into the bar to buy a beer. Startled by how dim the place was, I bumped into one of the men playing pool before my eyes adjusted. When I mut-tered an apology, he said something in Spanish and the other player laughed. At the bar the bartender and a patron arm-wrestled, grunting in Spanish. On the television was a boxing match, also in Spanish. Span-ish-language versions of beer and chewing-tobacco posters covered the wall.

Displaced and a bit daunted, I'd have walked out if I hadn't really wanted a beer. After two years of college Spanish, I'd retained barely enough to order food in Mexican restaurants. Let's see, *Dime una cer-veza.* Maybe I ought to just say *cerveza.* Or just *Fal-staff.*

I waited politely at the end of the bar and watched the arm-wrestling match, which the patron quickly won. The bartender patted him on top of the head, opened the rickety cash register, and handed over a twenty. Then he turned, looked at me and raised his eyebrows.

"A beer," I stammered.

"¿Que?"

Oh, hell. "Um, *una cerveza.*"

"No, kid. I mean, what kind?"

The victorious patron snickered as he folded the twenty into the brim of his cowboy hat, looking down at the bar.

I chugged a Miller and left.

Bob hadn't managed to scare up any ice cream. "I was really in the mood for it, too," he said. "I found a woman over there, but she didn't have a key."

He touched some stress points on the motor, decided they were cool enough, and drove El Basurero out of the Middle of Nowhere. I turned around in the front seat in time to see the green sign that read NUTT. POPULATION: 3.

"Did you get a beer," Bob asked.

"Yeah." Across a vast plain of scrub trees, renegade grasses, miles beyond the power lines supplying the juice for Nutt's single television set, I watched the Cookes Range drift dreamily by.

                                       Back on the interstate—I-10 now—at a rest area halfway between Deming and Lordsburg, we stopped for dinner. The only food left in the car was peanut butter (brought all the way from Oxford), grape jelly (New Orleans) and eight slices of Wonder Bread (Des Moines). An hour before sunset we sat at a stone parkbench, eating triple-decker peanut butter sandwiches and drinking lukewarm instant iced tea (Bob's contribution, also all the way from Oxford). In this task we employed plastic cutlery purchased in Gatlinburg and a cocktail glass stolen from a bar in Chicago. After dinner, at the confluence of the rest area on-ramp and the interstate, we crossed the Continental Divide.

As with all attractions which advertise themselves exclusively on interstate billboards, one can never be precisely sure when one becomes aware of The Thing. I must have seen twenty of the signs before I read the first aloud: "THE THING! WHAT IS IT?!?!"

"It's only seventy-nine miles away now," Bob countered. "I saw the first one of those back when it was in the one-sixties."

The next sign, just four miles ahead, exclaimed, THE THING! PREHISTORIC MYSTERY? On each sign there was some sort of ?-and-!-bedecked teaser for whatever it was The Thing was, appendaged by variables like "Genuine Indian Moccasins," "Soft-Serve Ice Cream" or "Free Pepsi with Fill-up." Bob and I leaned forward in our seats, trying to be the first to read the next Thing sign aloud. We'd watched the signs for so long, counted down their miles and recorded their contents, that it seemed sweetly impossible that, near the Arizona state line, there it was, right off the exit. THE THING? was emblazoned in 15-foot letters across the side of a corrugated-aluminum one-story barn. THE THING? was also painted across the roof of the gift-shop, a cluttered and rather nondescript A-frame. An American flag flew near the gaspumps, and though we didn't yet need refueling, we never debated whether we ought to stop.

Clearly, The Thing? attracted fewer visitors than even Gatlinburg's most out-of-the-way knick-knack emporia. The giftshop had a dust-covered, en-trenched look to it: not only were they not selling too many giant plastic houseflies, they weren't even get-ting too many tourists to jostle or fondle them. We wandered the giftshop, enjoying the 60-degree air con-ditioning and searching for the best roadrunner statu-ette. My favorite, forged from bronze-look plastic, came with the kind of cheesy little thermometer morticians give you with their freebie desktop calendars. It only cost eight bucks.

We knew even before we'd left Oxford that these places were inevitably disappointments, but by now we'd learned to savor that disappointment. So as we queued up to pay our 75 cents and—to judge from the mild surprise that crossed the face of the pimply teenager who obligingly took our quarters—become the first people all day to take the self-guided back-lot tour that would send us Thingward, we didn't really care what was out there. "I just hope it's real bad," I said.

"So bad it's good," Bob added. "I'd bet on it. I am betting on it. I'm betting six bits, bubba."

"Oh, it is good," the teenager drawled. "People like it. There's a money-back garntee, butcept no one ever asked me for dime one since I been here."

What greeted us, along a white-striped sidewalk that connected a circular enclave of barns, sheds and carports, was a themeless, incoherent hodge-podge of exhibits: vintage farm implements next to 300-year-old paintings of cows, ersatz conestogas next to a jail cell full of life-size wooden likenesses of human beings being hanged, beheaded and generally tortured. A sign said the figures had been created by an area man, who'd employed no tool but a chainsaw, and proclaimed this display as the only of its kind in the world.

"Big surprise," Bob said. "I mean, who would *think* to do this? The guy couldn't have been a walking testimonial to mental hygiene."

The open-air sections of this makeshift museum were flanked by badly peeling stick-your-head-through paintings on 8-by-4 sheets of plywood, where I posed for a photo as a Bible-clutching pilgrim waif.

Then, around the corner, in the penultimate

shed, inside a glass-topped but otherwise humble casket lay a mummified pretty-much-human form, dressed in tattered clothes, and a sign said:

> THE THING
> 20,000 B.C.
> The thing is . . .
> NO ONE KNOWS
> JUST WHAT *THE THING IS!?!*

Bob scoffed. "20,000 B.C.? If in fact people were wearing clothing two hundred twenty-one centuries ago, I can't see how it could still be intact today." He studied the bier carefully, circling it, examining every angle. "Nice bonnet."

"Maybe it's not real," I said. "Maybe it's clay or wax or mud. What's that in its arms there, do you think?"

"Probably The Thing II. Its baby. Soon to provide tourism to a future generation."

We returned to El Basurero. The moon shone less brightly than the night before, but we set sail, undaunted, for Tucson.

11
Wild
in the
Country

For most of my childhood my maternal grandparents lived in Jacksonville, Illinois, and for two weeks every summer my sister and I were dispatched to visit them. Though it was an enjoyable ritual, I was never quite at ease.

Granted, the glories were many. Jacksonville had cable television as early as 1965—a marvel which wouldn't reach Bryan, Ohio, for another fifteen years—and my grandparents' set had a remote control, something my parents still don't have. The neighborhood kids, all older, were five budding thugs who let me help them lob rocks off train overpasses. And Grandpa Bob, the sales manager at Cox Buick-Pontiac, allowed me to use the interior of new Rivieras as jungle gyms, introduced me to grownups as if I were an esteemed colleague and, once every visit, left work early to take me to a St. Louis Cardinals game.

But I found it difficult to get along with my grandmother for so long a visit. Shari and I called her "Mimi," the result of an apocryphal incident in which, while she was paddling my three-year-old butt, I supposedly chanted "Mean! Mean! Mean!" which eventually was shortened to "Mimi." To her, anything was better than "Grandma."

Mimi and I weren't always at odds. In all fairness, I was a willful troublemaker, and I couldn't have expected everyone to find that as amusing as Grandpa Bob did. He was a reformed gambler and a recovering alcoholic. He quit gambling because he could cheat too well, and had attended two Alcoholics Anonymous meetings every week since 1955. He'd had four heart attacks, but his recovery from them was complete. What finally caught up to him was smoking. *Emphysema.* We used to send cassette tapes to each other, sports reports chocked with free associations about Johnny Bench and Diego Segui, Ernie Banks and Mudcat Grant; we had to stop when he couldn't talk for more than ten minutes without running short of breath. He lost his job because of it, moved to Bryan for a year, and finally, in desperation, joined that long line of aged, infirm Americans seeking clean, thin, dry air in what was once the Gadsden Purchase. He died a slow, painful death, trying to breathe with only seven percent of his lungs.

"How long ago did he die," Bob asked.

"Two years. Mom thought Mimi would have a hard time. And she did at first. Mom said she had to teach her how to balance a checkbook."

We passed the Prince Road exit, and I knew we'd gone way too far. "I think I missed it," I said.

Bob grunted in disgust and began flipping through the map. "How lost are we? What's the next exit?"

"Rustraff Road. Two miles."

"God. Are you sure you were ever here?"

I'd messed up, for what seemed the hundredth time since Denver. I would've sworn I-10 went right through Tucson, like I wanted, but we were somewhere on the outskirts. "Do you see Speedway on there? If we can find Speedway, I'm almost totally sure it intersects with Pantano. That's what she told me to look for: Pantano."

Bob found Speedway on the map and directed us back through Tucson, certainly the longest route possible, and we finally arrived at my grandmother's condo complex, Villa Serenas.

"I thought they had water shortages out here," Bob said. "Somewhere in this town, dehydrated illegal aliens are dying so that this fountain may so copiously spray."

The fountain was spectacular, lit with slate blues and peacock greens, great blooms of water that evaporated in the night sky—a frighteningly ostentatious apparatus for a cluster of retirement condos.

At the walled, barred, television-monitored front gate, we buzzed Mimi's apartment. "Hi. It's Mark. See." Bob and I waved at the security camera as it panned past us.

A buzzer sounded as the gate popped open, and she met us halfway through the courtyard. She and I embraced. "You made good time," she said.

"Yeah, I guess," I said. We'd made terrible time.

Villa Serenas was pretty opulent, more than my grandparents could really afford, though budgeting was neither's strong suit. There was a pool, a jacuzzi, a sauna, an exercise room and ten tennis courts— none of which were used even once by Mimi or Grandpa Bob. I expected her place to look empty inside without Grandpa Bob around, but she'd redecorated it in a smart, contemporary style. With neither a wheelchair nor an oxygen tank in sight, it was on the lee side of spacious.

She turned down the volume on Johnny Carson and asked about our trip. I'd left out Truth or Consequences altogether, and Bob was amusing her with his account of The Thing when Mimi abruptly snatched up the remote control and turned up the volume. "They show one of these every night," she said, pointing at the screen. "Right after the 'Tonight Show.' I think they're neat."

Bob and I turned to watch the rock video for "Hold Me Now," the current single from a band called the Thompson Twins. Percussionist Alannah Currie's head was shaved well over her ears and bassist Joe Leeway's was bedecked in dreadlocks. Lead singer Tom Bailey sported a long red ponytail and an impeccably disheveled hairdo two parts mousse, one part dye, and one part chutzpah. All were dressed outlandishly in thrift-shop chic but the song is melodic and I'd have been surprised but not astonished if she had admired it after hearing it on the radio.

Throughout the video, she beamed, tapping both feet. By the end of the song, she was softly singing along. "I love that one," she said. "That's one of my favorites. Do you boys like videos?"

Bob and I, each of whom owned the album, nodded.

More than any American city I know, the names of the main streets in Tucson tell you everything you need to know about the forces at work there. To an extent, this is true everywhere. Every Southern city, for example, has a Lee Road, Drive or Highway. Washington, D.C.'s, plethora of letters, numerals and states tell you it's a planned city. Bryan, Ohio's, two principal thoroughfares are High Street and Main Street—a fair indictment of the town's general failure of imagination.

Tucson, though, has it all over those places. The Spanish and Mexican influence dwells along the curbs of Tanque Verde Road, Valencia Road, Pantano Road and Camino Seco. Gringo blandness bubbles merrily down Kolb Road, Stone Avenue, Roger Road and Craycroft Road. The enduring military presence takes in Fort Lowell Road, which leads to historical old Fort Lowell, as well as Aviation Highway, which leads to Davis-Monthan Air Force Base. For the influx of retirees, try either Country Club or Golf Links roads. Transplanted Eastern money seems responsible for the intersection of Broadway and Park, while the legacy of the frontier padres can be found on Mission Road, St. Mary's Road, Oracle Road and Miracle Mile. The area's desperate dependence on irrigation is spelled out in green-and-white on Wetmore Road, Sweetwater Drive, and Flowing Wells Road.

Nearly all of these are called *roads,* or *drives* or *ways,* and that's what nearly all of them are. *Avenues* and *courts* and *boulevards* would seem inappropriate out here in the desert, where we were far, far from home.

Still: next to an Exxon station on Speedway, we found a massive display of Elvis tapestries.

The next day, while Bob wrote postcards by the pool, Mimi asked me to sit down. "Hold out your hand," she said, and pressed a crisp $100 bill into my palm. "This was Bob's last insurance hundred. I want you to keep it."

Insurance hundreds, Grandpa Bob had explained years ago, were good things to have. If you had an insurance hundred tucked away in your wallet and, for instance, you got arrested, that bill would buy $1,000 in bail money. Grandpa Bob spent many an insurance hundred.

"The last one," she said. "Now, don't just spend it. You hang onto this until you really need it. I hope you won't ever really need it, but if you do, you'll have it. Just hang onto this, all right?"

We talked about Grandpa Bob for a half hour. Mimi told me about their courtship, and in particular about her attempt to make Grandpa Bob jealous during a high school after-game dance. Grandpa Bob, the starting halfback, had played well, and he celebrated by getting drunk and flirtatious. Irked, Mimi left with Sam Little, to go neck in his Dusenberg. After a few minutes, Sam abruptly grabbed the back of Mimi's head and shoved it toward the seat.

For an awful moment, I was terrified my grandmother was about to tell me an oral sex story.

It turned out that Sam had seen his rival coming and was afraid of being spotted. But Grandpa Bob suspected nothing, having come out in the parking lot only to urinate, which he did, on the front grill of Sam's car. "He never knew we were in there," Mimi said.

I studied my grandmother's face. I had no trouble imagining what she'd looked like in high school: fair, pretty, reckless and independent. I kissed her on the cheek.

When Bob came in to shower up for dinner, Mimi produced a huge glass jar full of American coins. "Your Grandpa Bob saved these," she said. She set the jar beside the dinner table, then rummaged in a kitchen drawer until she found several paper coinroll containers. "He would always dump change in this jar after work, or any time he came home with it. When he was drinking, of course, he'd store it up until it was enough for another bottle. After that he'd use it for mad money. Now, I'll tell you what."

She paused long enough that Bob and I were required to say, "What?"

"I want you to take these to Las Vegas and hit the jackpot for me. Will you do that? You boys can just roll these coins up, and then you can have 'em. You're still planning to go to Vegas, aren't you?"

Yes, we told her, we were.

"Well, then, you take this money to blow in Vegas. But if you hit the jackpot, you have to promise to call me. Is that a deal?"

Bob and I mounted a feeble protest, mostly out of courtesy, but Mimi insisted.

"If you don't hit the jackpot," she said, happier than I could ever remember seeing her, "then you can just send me a postcard."

After we'd finished rolling the jarful of coins, we counted out $83.77.

Mimi squealed blissfully. "I'm so glad there's so much," she said. "Now you two have a stake for Vegas. Your Grandpa Bob would *love* it."

Bob looked at the illuminated fifty-foot replica of an Easter Island stone idol. On the observation deck, at the crown of the great head, two tykes posed for a picture. "This isn't Oxford, Ohio."

"Nope," I said. "This isn't Oxford at all."

We walked past the statue of an orange longhorn steer into the clubhouse. "I think I saw Buddha," Bob said.

"You did. He's right next to the Sphinx and the Sun God."

As we paid our greens fees and chose our balls—periwinkle for me, puce for Bob—we asked the girl behind the counter if she knew when Tucson's Magic Carpet Golf was built.

"1962, I think." Her name was Cath, and she was a couple years younger than us. "Somebody told me once."

The last lines of text on the scorecard rules read, "Skill and fun for everyone! (You can't beat fun)."

A huge, hairy spider dangled over the cup of the first hole. Bob made me go first. "That makes sense—1962," I said. "I'm pretty sure I read somewhere that the Southwest is where blotter acid came from." My putt evaded the spider's nine legs, but lipped out. I sank the two-putt.

"This isn't Oxford," Jim said, looking past the spider to the 25-foot monkey astride a nearby hole.

America has scores of wacky putt-putt courses—many of which we'd passed on the outskirts of Gatlinburg—but Tucson's Magic Carpet Golf is a true original. Though it's more elaborate than most, what really sets Magic Carpet Golf apart from the pretenders is that here the ostriches and octopi, alligators and tyrannosaurus rexes, castles and snakepits, pygmy huts and Spanish galleons are less hazards than scenery. The Easter Island hole, for example, is nothing more than a straight putt through the 8-foot high, 6-foot wide mouth of the idol. To succumb to this "hazard," you'd have to be weirded-out by the very idea of tapping a fluorescent golf ball through a gaping orifice in a stone head four stories high.

Tucson isn't really a tourist town. Twenty years ago it might've been, but today people don't so much *visit* here as *winter* here. Consequently, industries catering to the semipermanent tourists—country clubs and expensive restaurants—are on the wax. On the wane is Magic Carpet Golf, which for all its charm could use a coat of paint.

We played pretty well the first eighteen, at least as maiden putt-putt rounds go. My worst hole was Skull, which took me five. But Bob took six angry strokes in and round Buddha's genitals, and I won the round, 46–49. Par, of course, is 36.

On the second eighteen, Bob overcame a triple-bogey on Goop and capitalized on my misfortune at the ineffable Holes of Confusion to eke it out, 47–48.

On the last hole I won a free game by ringing a bell in a plaster cobra's mouth.

In the clubhouse we bought Dr. Peppers from a machine. A guy named Dan sat beside Cath behind the counter, washing golf balls. They'd seen the plates on El Basurero, and asked what brought us from Ohio to Magic Carpet Golf. Once again Bob and I did a song-and-dance that made people wish they were us. Cath was fascinated and insisted we draw a map, which Bob did. We autographed it and she tacked it to their bulletin board. We asked them to autograph our scorecards, and Cath's signature concluded with an exclamation mark. Above it, she drew a little kitten head.

I asked if she could recommend a good place for a few drinks. It was near midnight, the course was empty, and I was hoping she'd come along. "Dallas," she said. "That's the place to go. The bar Dallas, not the city Dallas. The bar Dallas is just up Speedway, about six or seven blocks. Actually, the best place to go was Dooley's, over by the U of A campus, but it got torched."

"The music sucks at Dallas," Dan said. "They play Journey *and* Willie Nelson, if you can believe that. There's no place to hear good rock 'n' roll in this town."

"Yeah," Cath said. "Dallas used to be better. I never go there anymore."

As we pulled into the Villa Serenas parking lot,

a radio station started to play Bruce Springsteen's *Born in the U.S.A.* album, which was released that same day. I turned off the ignition and Bob lit a cigarette. We listened to the whole thing in silence. I remembered seeing Springsteen a few years before in Cleveland, and the story he told about his first American tour. When Bruce stopped in Memphis, he took a cab to Graceland. He wanted to meet Elvis, just to say he was a big, big fan. Bruce jumped the fence and ran for the mansion on the hill. Security guards cut him off—"they told me Elvis was sleepin.' " Afterward, Springsteen said, he realized "it was probably just as well that I didn't get to see him. It's like, the man could have never lived up to my dreams about Elvis."

The album playing on the radio closed with "My Hometown," a song about how rootedness, no matter how bleak, is inevitably more life-affirming than transience, no matter how romantic. Bob finished a third cigarette. A continent away, I missed Bryan, Ohio.

There is Tucson, where my grandmother lives with thousands of other retirees as well as a full complement of people associated with the University of Arizona. And then there is South Tucson, where my grandmother will not go because she fears non-Caucasians without white-collar jobs and a mastery of spoken English. And there is Old Tucson—across the Ajo Mountains from the other two Tucsons—where John Wayne spent many a dusty shoot, where tourists now go to watch choreographed gunfights on the half hour, where sharp-eyed movie buffs can see a storefront facade which appeared in the corner of the frame at the beginning of the second reel of *Rio Bravo*.

El Basurero chugged up the pass through the Ajos, and around a saguaro- and prickly-pear bordered bend was the establishing shot for half the westerns I've ever seen. In the middle of a vast sage-bedecked basin was a cluster of buildings. A settlement. For as far as the eye could see—which must have been 30 miles—there were no power lines and only a single paved road.

Bob was shocked by the admission price. "Twelve dollars? Twelve *dollars?* I mean, do you really want to do this? For twelve dollars, we could play a day's worth of Magic Carpet Golf. For twelve dollars, we could do a lot."

"Yeah, well. We're here. Let's see it. We haven't had to pay for food for a while, right?"

He shrugged, then handed a twenty to the cowpoke who, resplendent in chaps, manned the turnstile.

Shots pierced the tranquility of the Arizona morn, and we scrambled for a place in the crowd lining Front Street. We hadn't missed much. A tussle outside the Front Street Saloon led inevitably to outlaws bouncing off corrugated rooftops into horse troughs, to the gratuitous bullet-riddling of a perfectly harmless Stetson, first from the head of the ineffectual sheriff, then shot by shot, 6 feet by 6 feet, across the street. The sheriff's long-lost brother appeared from a dust cloud, gave a pair of Colt revolvers a half-dozen spins each and then methodically plugged the desperadoes square in their vile hearts.

We two hundred tourists applauded.

Beside Bob and me, a gray-haired man dressed in tennis duds turned to his small grandson. "Didn't you like that, Justin? Wasn't that wonderful?"

The boy nodded, but he seemed only marginally impressed. "Yeah. It was pretty neat, I guess."

The grandfather beamed. "You know, that's what movies were like when I was your age."

"Oh," the boy said. "Was that before the first *Star Wars?*"

Nothing was being filmed at Old Tucson. On the back-lot choo-choo ride, we saw the hacienda that had been the main set for "The High Chaparral," a show I'd watched when I was eight, memorable for the weekly slaughter of Indians by the cattle barons. The train guide—a sonorous-voiced old man with gunmetal hair who was dressed as a frontier undertaker—pointed out ponds into which Kirk Douglas had been thrown, railroad tracks upon which Jeannette Nolan had been tied. He spewed forth the names of forgettable series and movies. Twice he mentioned Joe Namath.

We rode past a standard-issue wooden fort into a courtyard, where a demolished police cruiser was parked next to a dry fountain. "Ladies and gentlemen, you all just missed the big excitement," the guide said. "Right here, just a few months ago, they filmed a fight scene from Burt Reynolds's new movie, *Cannonball Run II.*"

"No way," Bob muttered. "They aren't making a sequel of that."

But, yes, they were, and they did. Burt Reynolds—whose first exposure to Old Tucson was his role of halfbreed blacksmith Quint Asper in "Gunsmoke"—had brought with him such prototypical Western stars as Dom Deluise, Sammy Davis, Jr., Jim Nabors and Washington Redskins quarterback Joe Theismann, in order to film a scene from a car-race movie in which there would be no filmed car race.

As a movie set, Old Tucson is unlikely to usurp much glory from the California studios. At one point

165

in the late fifties, there were more than thirty prime-time Westerns on television; when we visited Old Tucson there were none. The last, "Father Murphy," was indeed filmed partially at Old Tucson—but NBC scheduled the show opposite "60 Minutes" and the only people who ever saw it were a troop of Alaskan Cub Scouts whose portable set couldn't quite pull in CBS's Anchorage affiliate.

On the soundstage tour, the rightful centerpiece was the fading set of the Long Branch Saloon—where Miss Kitty once glided down the stairs and many an outlaw was battered with breakaway chairs and glucose bottles. But more visitors reserved their rapt ogling for the exact replica of Frank Sinatra's Las Vegas office, used to film his cameo for *Cannonball Run II*.

That night, our last in Tucson, Mimi took us to Pizza Hut. Even before the second pitcher arrived, she was loopy with drink. And she was great fun.

She told us about her new job as a seamstress for a neighborhood fabric outlet. She told us about a new friend she'd made, a woman named Lois with whom she'd purchased season tickets for the university's drama series. She mentioned, in passing, two men she'd recently dated.

"That's great," I said. "Really great."

"Yeah," Bob said, amused and impressed.

My grandmother seemed stuffed with life. For the first time since Grandpa Bob had died, she went a whole hour without talking about him. And when she finally did, it was without sadness or sentiment: a slapstick tale of his utter lack of knowledge about the automobiles he'd sold for a quarter-century. "The only people he sold to were dummies who didn't know any more about them than Bob did. Yes. Or people who bought his line of bull. That's right. Bob knew *nothing* about cars. No sir. Never learned a *thing* about them. *I* knew more about cars than he did."

I felt yet another point of connection with my Grandpa Bob—the man who taught me baseball, orneriness and a fundamental tenacity. I thought about my Grandpa Bob's final insurance hundred, now tucked in my wallet.

We finished the pizza, went back to Mimi's condo, packed up and got ready, once again, for a nocturnal drive through the Great American Desert. Still a tad tipsy, Mimi lodged a feeble protest.

"We're only going to Phoenix," I assured her.

"My brother lives there," Bob said. "He's expecting us."

"Well. Okay, boys. But promise me this: promise me you'll call me right away if you strike it rich in Vegas. With those coins, I mean. Will you promise me that?"

We said we would.

She shook Bob's hand goodbye. As she hugged me, she whispered, "Do you have that hundred?"

"Yes," I whispered back.

"Remember, that's just for emergencies, okay?"

"Okay."

Outside the front gate of Villas Serenas, a sprinkler head had exploded, sending a steady jet of water into the night, a jet more powerful if less intricate than the nearby fountain. Bob and I were drenched as we leapt through it. Behind us a spotlight produced a rainbow, and Maude Agnes Roberts Reschar bade us to drive with care.

12
Viva
Las Vegas

Scarcely back on the interstate, the lights of Tucson receding through El Basurero's filthy rear window, Bob cleared his throat and told me this might well be the end of the road.

I had thought we'd left this sort of talk behind in Estes Park. We were on our Western leg now, happy, committed and rolling. In the passenger's seat, I rummaged through Bob's attaché case, searching hopelessly for a tape we hadn't already listened to. Maybe I'd heard him wrong.

But no. Just before dinner, while I was in the shower, he'd called his mother collect just to say calamity hadn't yet fatally befallen us. His mother told him that some mail had come from the university where he'd planned to transfer that fall, swayed primarily by a $6,000 poetry fellowship he'd been awarded. She read Bob the letter, which said he had not, in fact, received the fellowship.

We shot through the desert in silence for a thick five minutes. Bob was visibly shaken.

Finally I found something to say. "This may

sound crazy, but I think the best thing you can do is forget it."

Bob kept his eyes on the road and bit his lip.

"Seriously," I said. "First of all, it's probably some bureaucratic screw-up. It's not like there's anything you can do about it now, so you might as well not let it eat at you."

Bob just shook his head.

"No, I'm really serious." I turned in the seat to face him. "Look, some guy told you on the phone that you'd won it, right? Okay, so it only stands to reason that they're more likely to have messed up that letter than to have messed up a phone call. Probably just a wrong-envelope kind of deal."

Again the head shake.

"Really, I mean, you don't have a thing to gain by stewing in it. You can call them from your brother's and raise hell and all that, straighten it right out." I took a deep breath and studied Bob's face, trying to decide if I was making him angry. I forged ahead anyway. "And even if you didn't get it, you might as well have a good time for the rest of the summer."

He took a breath as if he were about to speak, then stopped himself.

"Okay," I said, scrambling to cover myself. "If you really didn't get it—and I'll bet, I'll really *bet* you did—but if you didn't, going back to Ohio isn't going to bring it back."

Bob reached for the tapedeck volume knob and turned it up. "If this is true," he muttered under the music, "if I don't get that money, the trip is over."

An answer to that didn't suggest itself. I checked the map. We were headed northwest toward Phoenix. The right direction, I thought, leaning my head against the window to take a nap, filled with dumb optimism, manifest destiny and too much beer.

Between Bob and his older brother Bill there throbbed some unresolved antagonisms, which I could glimpse behind their forced politeness. We made it to Phoenix by two, and Bill was awake when Bob called for directions. When we got there, Bill insisted we go to a nearby Denny's for a snack—in the same overeager way that a college freshman chooses for his visiting parents a restaurant where he won't be recognized. By now I'd found enough of a second wind to catch what lurked below their chitchat: Bill's bullying one-upmanship, Bob's chilly maintenance of old grudges.

I woke the next morning near noon. In the living room, Bob leafed through the yard-high stack of *Penthouse* magazines while Bill trotted out his possessions: stereo equipment, pool toys, antigravity exercise machinery and a thin, toothsome young girlfriend named Laresa.

We spent the day swimming, sunning and snacking. That night Bill took us to a nearby bar, where he destroyed us not only on the billiard table but on each of the three video games. Bob let his older brother get what kicks he could from ritual slaughter without allowing him the juicier pleasure of seeing his younger brother give a damn.

Grilling up a heap o' grub for lunch the next day had been Bill's idea, although somehow, in our trek to the Safeway for supplies, we wound up paying. But no matter. I'd pretty much forgotten about it by the time we sat down with our sliced tomatoes and our onion rings and our corn on the cob and our American beer and our cheeseburgers—

splendidly rare, mine with the works and Bob's, as always, plain.

After lunch I waddled back to the pool, popped a cold one and sprawled myself across the deck, content to pick corn from my teeth and contract a mild sunburn.

Bob woke me with a soft kick to my ribs and said the fellowship snafu had been resolved.

"Oh, yeah?" I tried to act surprised, and knew better than to tell him I'd told him so.

"It's a long story," he said. "Basically, it was a clerical error."

"Really?"

Bob seemed strangely disappointed. Here we were, on the final third of our journey, and nothing particularly horrible had happened yet.

"Vegas?" he said.

"Vegas," I confirmed.

"I always wanted to spend Christmas in Las Vegas," Bob said, waving goodbye to his brother as El Basurero pulled out of the driveway.

"You're diseased," I said, smiling, delighted to leave Phoenix with our spirits and expectations risen from the ashes.

Had we made this trip thirty years earlier—in 1954, say—our principal thoroughfare would have been the late, lamented Route 66, subject of a hepcat TV show and at least one wistful photo-obituary in every major American magazine. In Mojave County, Arizona, east of Kingman and north of the Hulalapai Mountains, 66 miles northeast of London Bridge, we crossed one of the final extant stretches of the road that made America safe for tourism—named, in honor of Kingman's character-actor and native son, Andy Devine Boulevard.

Behind the wheel, I felt compelled to exit I-40, the superhighway that has superseded Route 66. "We have to do this," I said as Bob arched an eyebrow. "Don't you want to tell your kids you drove down Andy Devine Boulevard? And, besides, I'm thirsty and the cooler's empty."

Bob shrugged. "Okay. Let's give the car a drink, too."

So we procured beverages at an air-conditioned Big Boy, leaving our rusty steed parked across Andy Devine Boulevard in the only available shade: the long shadow cast by a rectangular delivery van painted the same shades of blue and gold as a Cub Scout uniform.

When we returned, the van's short, pot-bellied owner was adjusting the tire pressure on the mini-bike mounted to his rear bumper. He approached us with the unassuming friendliness of a lonesome traveler and introduced himself as "Crazy Reb." He'd converted this delivery van, once a wine truck, into a motorhome complete with a tiny bathroom. His time, he told us, was divided between panning for gold in the streams of the Sierra Nevadas near Fresno, where he was coming from, and panning for gold in the streams of the Ozarks in northwestern Arkansas, where he was headed. "There's more gold in Arkansas than you'd think."

Crazy Reb wore a cap, blue jeans and a "Texxas Jam '83" T-shirt that listed, on the back, the bands who'd played, from Ted Nugent to ZZ Top and Molly Hatchet. I'd guess he was in his midforties. He had thick hair on the back of his neck and one bushy eyebrow, under which he squinted. His raspy voice was hard to take seriously because of a lisp that gave him trouble with his *R*'s, a bit more afflicted than Barbara Walters and a bit less than Elmer Fudd.

As Bob and I ministered to El Basurero—adding oil, pouring water over the engine block—Crazy Reb continued to talk. At first I'd written him off as an engaging crackpot, but then he began to tell us about how he'd spent the '60s, when he'd opened the first youth hostel in Haight-Ashbury and had a first-hand view of all that was flower power. "Those kids had good ideas, good principles, and I still live by 'em. Love your fellow man and whatnot. But the drugs. Let me tell you, the drugs ruined a lot of the best minds of that generation." He said he was instrumental in soliciting the first drug-counseling money spent by the city of San Francisco and, for several years after that, worked as a drug counselor. As he discussed San Francisco in the '60s and '70s, his voice quieted, and there was no doubting him.

His transition to UFO talk was invisible. He claimed to have seen four, but only one up close, his first sighting, in Arkansas. "It swooped right down. It was beautiful, and it hovered not twenty feet over my head for onto a half hour. Very bright colors. Some I'd never seen before." After that, he took up the habit of jerking his head to the night sky, looking for more UFO's. "That's why they got to callin' me Crazy Reb." He grinned, and had a nice smile. "I don't mind. It's in good fun. And I know they're up there."

From the driver's side door of the van he released his mongrel puppy—a homely little beast that was every bit as friendly as its owner. We petted it while Crazy Reb told us about Robert Redford. "I've met up with him four times in the last eighteen months, just pure coincidence, you might say, but I guess that's how most good things happen. Camping. You know. Redford he's quite the outdoorsman."

Bob asked what they discussed.

Crazy Reb beamed. "Well, you're not going to believe this, but I swear to God, we talked about UFO's. That's my special interest, of course, but Redford seemed awfully interested in them, too. He asked me a lot of questions about my first sighting, that close one."

"So," I said, "Robert Redford believes in UFO's, huh?" By mistake, a note of condescension crept into that, and I was happy Crazy Reb missed it.

"Well, he never exactly said, not right out. The famous have to guard their opinions, you understand. Their lives, I can tell you, aren't like yours and mine. But one time I just right out and asked him. 'Reb,' he says, 'I been listenin' to you all this time, haven't I?' See, he more or less squirmed out of that, but if I were a betting man, and I'm not, I'd have to bet that, yes. Sure. Robert Redford, he believes in 'em. Ha. Yep. Believes in 'em."

But then the conversation took a sorry turn. "I believe we're living in the final days," Reb said, "I sincerely do. All the signs are in place." He claimed he wasn't a religious man and, like others who lay that claim, immediately started quoting from the Scriptures. Distracted, I watched truckers and tourists thunder down Andy Devine Boulevard.

Crazy Reb cajoled us into his wine truck, and showed us photographs of a fountain in San Francisco—a feature of which, Reb said, fulfilled a prophesy of Micah or Habakkuk. Inside of the truck it must've been 390 degrees, and it smelled like rotting wool. The photos were blurry, overexposed shots of wet marble.

"Ah," Bob and I said, barely out of synch, as Reb passed us one after another.

We each petted his mutt a final time, shook his hand and wished him luck finding gold, UFOs and Robert Redford in Arkansas.

A crazy quest, Reb's. Or so I thought until we found Elvis Presley in Santa Claus, Arizona.

Santa Claus is a little roadside place on the west shoulder of U.S. 93, which exists to carry tourists back and forth from Phoenix to Las Vegas. We nearly missed it. In fact, we did miss it. The cluster of three tiny ramshackle A-frames painted to resemble peppermint candies hadn't been advertised on any billboards, and since I had El Basurero doing a cool 70, I overshot the parking lot and had to make a dusty U-turn.

"This'll be great," I said, and I thought it would be—a crass and charming idea for a tourist trap or haven, this Christmas decoration and seasonal trinketry shop in the Arizona desert. But it was on its last legs. Styrofoam silver bells, strands of burned-out Christmas lights and faded plastic likenesses of Old Saint Nick garnished this little village. A lopsided, artificial twenty-foot tree whistled in the wind beside a broken Coke machine and an empty ice freezer. Two of the three buildings were padlocked; through their windows, encrusted with layers of sand and decade-old aerosol snow, Jim and I saw dusty, overturned fiberglass statuettes of elves and reindeer. Alongside the SANTA CLAUS, ARIZONA/ESTABLISHED 1937 sign was another: FOR SALE BY OWNER/$52,500/INQUIRE AT GIFTSHOP. An arrow pointed the way. "We ought to buy it," I said, "and skip graduate school."

The giftshop stocked no seasonal items. Its shelves were littered with flea-market knickknacks at antique-shop prices. Battered paperbacks cost a buck. What little money the place generated must have come from the short-order grill and the soft-drinks cooler. On a stool behind the countertop cash register, a haggard, fiftyish man looked up from his circle-the-word puzzle and asked if we needed anything.

"Just looking around," I said.

"Postcards, maybe," Bob offered, heading for the rack near the pop cooler.

We found no outstanding buys in the postcard rack or among the "collectables" nearby.

On a radio tuned to a Las Vegas station, a commercial was plugging the new Eddie Murphy comedy album. Suddenly we heard him doing his Elvis Presley impersonation. "Le-mon-ade," Murphy sang to peals of laughter. "Bay-bee, bring me some le-mon-ade."

Astonished, Bob and I looked at one another, and in unison said, "Give us this day our daily Elvis."

I restrained from dropping to my knees to thank Santa.

The last time I'd been in Las Vegas, I left behind a front tooth.

I was ten years old. My parents had won free VIP admission for four to Disneyland as a doorprize at an RV convention, and we were on our way back to Ohio from Southern California. When Dad suggested stopping in Las Vegas, I thought it was a pretty cool idea, unaware that the only entertainments open to my age group were the viewing of neon exteriors and the KOA campground swimming pool. So one night, while my mother and father were squandering two rolls of nickels in slot machines and $50 on a scatological Buddy Hackett dinner show, I was left in the campground to entertain myself and to babysit for my sister. We went to the pool, of course. For a few hours I amused myself by bombing Shari with a nifty series of cannonballs, melons and sitting preachers. When that finally chased her from the pool, crying and in search of her towel, I decided to experiment with a dive I'd seen the big kids do: a sailor dive, a headfirst plunge executed with the hands clasped behind the buttocks. I did it once, twice, three times, delirious from smacking my face on the surface and savoring the rush of water past my ears. And then I tried one in the shallow end, whereupon I knocked out my upper left incisor.

I'd always wanted a second chance at Vegas, when I was old enough to do every damn thing in town.

The first section Bob and I explored was not The Strip but an auxiliary corridor of decadence along Fremont Street, where we saw some casinos we'd heard of, like the Golden Nugget, and a huge neon cowboy I'd seen in a movie.

We pulled into a hotel that promised free parking for patrons of their casino. Naturally, the counter where parking vouchers were issued was in a hard-to-find hallway, necessitating a journey past more gambling opportunities than there are humans, dogs and hamsters in Bryan, Ohio. Our pockets swollen with a few rolls of Grandpa Bob's coins, we played along, dumping a couple bucks apiece into video poker machines.

"You know, that wasn't really all that much fun," I told Bob as we waited in a long line for our voucher.

"What?"

"Losing money. So why do all these people come from all over the planet to lose money?"

"Well, they come to win."

"But they almost all lose. Everyone knows that. I can't think of anything that isn't at least a little more fun than losing money. For two bucks I could've ridden a mechanical bull."

"Your grandmother gave us this money," Bob said, "for just this purpose. It's like a mission."

"Or a sentence. No, I'm just kidding. Let's go live it up and lose some more money."

On our way out we passed a sign advertising the night's entertainment: a new play starring TV's Gilligan, Bob Denver. An excerpt from a good review in the Needles, California, newspaper was included.

"Now," I said, "we're really having fun."

We ate dinner in an obscure, third-echelon casino. All the casinos offered cheap-eats as gambling ploys, but after a walk up and down Fremont we'd selected this one as the cheapest buffet of all: $2.95, all you can eat, including beverage.

The dinner, of course, was horrid. I chugged watery Diet Cokes and was hungry enough not to be put off by the lame food. But Bob ate lightly and even skipped dessert: small bowls of butterscotch pudding, clotted with unidentifiable lumps, of which I had seconds.

On the way out, Bob gambled. I explained why he shouldn't, but he had the bug.

He lost $2 in less than two minutes.

"There," I said. "Wasn't that fun?" Now I was the spoil-sport, hoarding Mimi's money in my pocket.

A sign across the street claimed THE LOOSEST SLOTS IN TOWN.

"Nudge, nudge," Bob said, "Wink, wink."

In a lucite case in the entryway to the Golden

Nugget, not 10 feet from the street, one million U.S. dollars in cash fluttered in the wind, looking rather like a television commercial for a lawnmower leaf attachment.

Back at the car, we shed dirty shorts and Hawaiian shirts in favor of rumpled dress shirts and long pants. I tightened my tie in the rearview mirror.

"I'm getting a little tired," Bob whined, "of changing clothes outside, all over America."

By now it was dark, and we drove along those gaudy, famous streets toward Paradise.

The Strip—or Las Vegas Boulevard, to trundle out its Christian name—is not in Las Vegas, but in the adjoining suburb of Paradise. Ah, sweet bird of euphemism.

We parked at the extreme northern cusp, in a set-up that would have been called a shopping center had it only contained a supermarket, a bank branch, a fabric shop, a Baskin-Robbins and a bakery thrift outlet instead of these souvenir stores and 25-cent adult-movie masturbation stalls. The main store—where, in the Midwest, the Kroger Sav-On would have stood—was called World's Largest Gift Store.

Anywhere else, the braggadocio and derision-potential of World's Largest Gift Store would have been irresistible. But a few blocks away, triangles of light refracted off a three-story geodesic dome and circus performers flew over the heads of dice-rolling insurance adjustors from Waco—and that's the direction calculated to exert the most pull.

Bob and I walked through each casino on the Strip, taking anything that was free, including about a dozen sweet highballs from plastic cups identical to those my doctor asks me to pee in.

A block off the Strip, we found a casino that, in honor of its eighth anniversary, was staging a free burlesque show at midnight. We discovered this at nine, and resolved to return. Until you've ogled G-strings, you're not in Las Vegas.

"I think this might be the only city in America that goes by its last name," Bob mused. "You never hear anyone talk about 'Angeles' or 'Diego' or 'Antonio' or 'Christi.'"

"Or 'York.'" I offered. "Or 'Orleans.'"

"Or 'Louis.' Or 'Moines.'" Bob took his time lighting a cigarette as he thought this over. "Vegas is the only one."

One casino congealed into another; the storied bright lights triggered a self-defensive bleariness. We dropped a few more of my grandmother's coins in several. Gambling must be more fun than it looks, I thought. Why, look! Look at all the people! This must be fun, just as a restaurant with a full parking lot must be good.

At every gambling juncture, the quarters slowly slipped away. In the Flamingo, I played the slots with dollar coins and was, at one point, $17 ahead—not much, granted, but a cooler head might have noted that $17 was 10 percent of the money I'd budgeted for food for the whole trip. Being ahead just $17 was no big deal, though, not even enough to brag about. Now $100, that would make a difference; no fortune, but enough to make me happy. I lost all my winnings, of course, in the fastest four minutes of my life, and dropped another $4 before my hand stopped reaching reflexively for the lever.

Beside me, Bob played video poker with quarters, doing well enough to walk away 75 cents wealthier.

I can't claim to have been entirely blasé about all of Vegas. A few things shook me, probably enough to produce facial expressions that would make any onlooker think, "Yeah, he's just in from the soybean patch."

Including:

1. In front of the Las Vegas Hilton, where Elvis Presley holds the attendance record in perpetuity, stood a billboard proclaiming the current attraction: Suzanne Somers, of TV's "Three's Company." Her mostly exposed breasts covered more square yards than my apartment. I stood on the sidewalk, my hands on my hips, imagining the frolicsome Miss Somers in rehearsal with thirty fawning male dancers named Darren, working together to mount a show worthy of the Elvis legacy. I prepared myself for a scream, but Bob dissuaded me. "Elvis should have never been in Las Vegas in the first place," said my friend.

2. In any random rest room, in any random casino, the individual toilet stalls are decorated, each with its own wallpaper, lamp and framed print. Because the lump-riddled butterscotch pudding hadn't agreed with me, I had the occasion to see a lot of Vegas restrooms. One even had princess telephones in the stalls.

3. Metal newspaper boxes—which back in the world as I'd known it, contained newspapers—here contain three-color brochures with such banner headlines as "Showgirls of Las Vegas," "Male Calls," "The Personal Touch," "Swinging Suzy's Escorts" and "Classy Lassies [Classy Lads Available]." Prominently on the cover of each brochure are Visa and Master-

card logos. One of these establishments listed its address as Industrial Road, in Suite A, billing itself as THE ONLY ESCORT SERVICE THAT LEAVES IT'S [sic] DOOR OPEN TO THE PUBLIC! Personally, I don't think one can ever be adequately prepared for ubiquitous newspaper boxes full of callgirl/callboy advertisements. I wasn't. I kept stopping to look at them, and decent folks stared—at me.

Twenty minutes before the burlesque show was slated to begin, Bob and I found the silliest of the many personal ads—for Brandy, who billed herself as a coed interested in issuing tutorials. Since the University of Nevada at Las Vegas was only a dozen blocks away, this was almost conceivable.

So I entered a phonebooth, on a fact-finding mission. For a quarter, I got to speak with Brandy her very self. Imagine: speaking with a prostitute in Las Vegas. Gary and Bev Winegardner's baby boy! Brandy spoke with a fake Texas accent, which at times lapsed into Brooklynese. She had space in her datebook that night, and told me that so long as I had a hotel room somewhere in Clark County—outside of the Las Vegas city limits—she would pay me a visit, for a courtesy fee of $100. There would be, she assured me, no hidden costs.

I asked her what subjects she was studying.

Languages seemed to be her specialty: French, English, Greek. She claimed to be assaying a broad-based course of study. You can always learn something new, she said. Every day is an education.

Sorry, I had to say. My room isn't in Clark County. It's in a 1967 Impala.

That was fun, I thought as I got out of the booth, preparing to tell Bob about Brandy. That conversation was worth a quarter, which might otherwise have entertained me at a slot machine for eleven seconds.

Bob and I were the first seated at the free burlesque show. A middle-aged brunette in a miniskirt showed us to a front-row table. Roughly the same size as a bowling-alley bar—with the small blue stage taking the place of the shoe-rental counter—the room filled slowly, affording us plenty of time to wonder what sort of a group we'd fallen in with. Our drinks arrived on our left just as five guys in shabby suits arrived on our right. I checked to see if the floor was sticky.

I needn't have worried. Eventually about a hundred people squeezed in, running the gamut from (behind us) a teenaged boy and girl with their parents to (at far left) a covey of smartly dressed grandmothers. The common bond among us, as we waited, was not sleaze but boredom.

The show, once underway, changed nothing. We endured a dreadful comic, a lame magician and two pretty gymnastic strippers just so we could say we'd done it, as if the risk had been taken from skydiving and we all wanted to do it anyway.

Bernie Allen, the comic, looked familiar. Bob thought so, too, but couldn't place him. Allen emcee'd the show, using jokes about farts and midgets as segues into the routines of Amber Corday and Sunny Day and "a very talented young magician, Mr. Scott Free."

Scott Free. I swear. He was the most insufferable sort of magician, the humorless kind, who widened his eyes to heighten suspense, brandished bouquets as if they were nitroglycerine, and spoke in a hush as if burdened by his reverence for a trade in which aluminum sabers are poked through boxed women and the seven of hearts is produced from an uncut orange. I helped Scott Free with that last bit, my first experience as "someone from the audience."

"Now examine this orange, Mark, and tell me if it's been tampered with in any way."

"Probably," I said. "Somehow. I just can't see it."

Scott was oblivious to my attempt at loosening him up.

I plucked a card from his deck and, as instructed, tore it into four pieces, which I did the wrong way, and Scott had to start over. The idea was that the reconstituted seven of hearts should appear in the center of the orange, but I inadvertently screwed *that* up when I halved the thing incorrectly, slicing off the lower left-hand corner of the card.

The crowd murmured. For my efforts, Scott gave me the card. The orange and the knife were whisked away by the lovely Sunny Day.

In their progress inward from (respectively) a multiplicity of Arabian veils and the petticoated raiments of a French farm girl down to their sequined G-strings, Amber and Sunny performed well enough to make me consider lust. Amber was much older than Sunny, and had to make up for that with more elaborate props. I rooted for the strippers to stay onstage forever, since only that would preserve me from Bernie Allen's stale one-liners.

"I know I've seen that guy before," Bob whispered. "Maybe in a movie."

"No way. In a *movie?* This guy? Not a chance."

"A guy with a duck on his head walks into a doctor's office," Bernie spat. "The doctor says, 'Can I help you?' and the duck says, 'Yeah. Get this guy off my ass.'"

There was little laughter, but no heckling either. People just didn't care. We were all going through the motions.

Bernie Allen thanked us for being a wonderful audience, somehow working into his closing the fact that he'd appeared in *Raging Bull.*

"My God," I said.

"I re*member* him!" Bob beamed. "When Robert De Niro was fat and trying to make it in all those dives, this guy played one of the other bad comics on the bill."

"Jesus. Bernie Allen As Himself."

Taped swing music signaled the end of the show and we filed out, a column of zombie communicants.

At about one-thirty we resumed casino hopping, trying to stay awake until breakfast, when we planned to eat a cheap meal and then drive to California. Past a four-story marquee embossed with a grotesque facsimile of Dean Martin's head, we wound up at the MGM Grand, where Bob gambled some more. I hadn't spent all of Mimi's coins, but I had decided to quit and, since she would never know any better, squander the remaining money on beer, fruit pies and admission to Disneyland.

As Bob drew to a video inside-straight, I noticed for the first time the sad obsessives, although they must have been present all along. These were people who had commandeered their own bank of slots, joylessly shuffling from machine to machine, inserting coins and pulling levers without pausing to see if they'd won. Several wore bathrobes, and one woman had her hair in curlers and a sleep mask dangling from her throat.

By the time I returned from another visit to a palatial bathroom, Bob, too, had ceased to have fun. "I'm $10.50 down for the night," he said. "Not counting the $2.95 buffet or the $3.50 for drinks at the burlesque show."

We sat in the lounge. On stage two men and two women slid through a set of slick country songs. The beers we ordered cost $3 apiece, and I thought Bob would kill me for having suggested them.

"You know what Las Vegas is," I asked. "I just figured this out. Las Vegas is prefab fun for adults who lack the imagination to put together a coherent vacation. This way, people don't have to have fun—they have Las Vegas. Lunkheads without any idea how to have fun as grown-ups don't have to worry about it. As long as there's Las Vegas, there's a swingin' time to be had, like it or not. It's like, vacant adults are forever absolved of the responsibility of having to create their own wild time. Vegas has done it for them."

"One size fits all," Bob said.

Six aging Golddiggers had deigned to join the lounge act for a few impromptu numbers. Women who had functioned for years as the butts of Dean Martin's sexist jibes now draped their arms around one another like camp counselors at the summer's final bonfire: tittering, bollixing lyrics, rocking from side to side, sending "New York, New York" out over the impervious heads of the sad obsessives.

We opted for the breakfast spread at the Holiday Inn. That the Las Vegas Holiday Inn was a casino might be disturbing only to me, but I register Holiday Inn as the place we go after late church, even though it's all the way up by the Turnpike, because it's an all-you-can-eat and Dad can really sock away the French toast. Or I think of it as the chain, founded in Memphis, in which Sam Phillips invested the wad he received upon selling Elvis Presley's contract to RCA and Col. Tom Parker. But in Las Vegas, the Holiday Inn is merely a second-echelon casino. Their $1.09 breakfast was only a few cents cheaper than nearby competitors.

My thighs ached as we went in. The streets were empty but every marquee continued to chew up the kilowatts. After forcing down as many cups of coffee as I could entice our waiter to pour, I still couldn't stay awake and—elbows on the table, fists propping up my head—slept with my nose poised over a plate of cold home fries.

Bob wrote a letter on the back of three placemats.

We walked outside into fierce daylight. Like newly charged felons avoiding news cameras, we shielded our eyes and limped back to El Basurero, the Strip having magically elongated itself overnight.

On our way out of town, at 3535 Las Vegas Boulevard, we passed the decidedly unimperial-looking Imperial Palace Hotel & Casino, which featured the show LEGENDS IN CONCERT: A MILLION-DOLLAR SHOW WITH MULTIMEDIA & LASER EFFECTS. A sign boasted UNBELIEVABLE RECREATIONS OF LEGENDARY SUPERSTARS. Very believable, however, was the first name on the list: Elvis, who in this depiction more closely resembled a zircon-cloaked Fred Flintstone, goofy on Quaaludes. Having suffered our daily Elvis, we led ourselves into temptation, onto I-15 toward the Magic Kingdom, eager for tourism of a purer stripe.

13

A Date with Elvis

We were hardly up to speed when El Basurero conked out, rolling to a stop with the rear axle in the Nevada desert and the front axle in the California desert. The car had died and come back to life so many times that I no longer could take this peril seriously, and Bob was less perturbed by this new automotive failure than he'd been by previous instances. He even posed for a picture, shinnying up the pole of the WELCOME TO CALIFORNIA sign, pretending to thump the daylights out of his head, but it was all for show. We joked and, once again, changed clothes outdoors as we calculated the distance to the City of Angels.

"Let's start this mother up." I grinned and turned the key.

Bob started to object, but was cut off by the motor's roar.

"Ha," I said. "California, here I come."

"We're in California already. All but the trunk."

        "God!" Bob shouted. "Wake up, will you!"

"I'm awake, I'm awake, I'm awake." I wanted to take us all the way into Los Angeles. That, I thought, would be an achievement.

"Wake *up!*" He pummeled me with our rolled-up map. "Let me drive."

"You've driven too much already. I ought to drive."

"Really, I won't utter a syllable of complaint—ever, I won't *ever* complain—if you just let me drive."

But I could not be swayed from my purpose, so as my eyelids sporadically slid closed, Bob tortured me with every item at his disposal. First he used the map, then he shot me with thin streams from his contact-lens fluid. Next it was handfuls of tepid water splashed from the cooler, followed by radio static at full volume. Occasionally Bob would sing an impromptu operetta in his demented falsetto. Throughout this barrage I slipped asleep from time to time—but never for very long, I argued, just long enough to produce a head-droop, a steering-drift and an I'm-awake-I'm-awake all-body convulsion. Bob was forced to employ all his tactics at once: the map-flog, the lens-cleaner water cannon, the splash from the cooler, the white noise and the panic-driven falsetto from hell.

"Well, okay," I said, pulling into a Mojave Desert rest area, still almost 100 miles from *Barstow* even. "Drive."

I woke up on the Santa Monica Freeway, very near Dodger Stadium. Bob was once again clubbing me with the map. "Figure out where in the name of Balboa we are," he ordered, "before one of these freeways runs us into the Pacific."

The first person we spoke to in California was a Canadian.

Bob and I were unshaven and unwashed, but we'd each found a towel that didn't stink and were walking toward Venice Beach, happy to have a place to take a nap and wait for Bob's friend Larry (our prospective host) to return from work. So when the curly-haired guy tapped us from behind, we were flat startled.

He smiled, introduced himself as Ray from Ontario and asked if we could point him in the direction of a singles bar he'd read about in *Playboy*.

"We're not from here," Bob apologized.

"Yeah," I admitted. "We're tourists." I was pleased, though, to have been taken for a local by someone who'd probably grown up not 200 miles from Bryan, Ohio.

"You should have been with me last night," Ray said. "Got plowed, arrested and everything."

"That can happen," Bob mused, "when you get plowed. I've heard tell. Sorry we missed it."

"Oh, you mean you don't drink? Eh, you're not like Mormons are you?"

"No," Bob said, bemused. "We're not anything like Mormons."

"Oh, right. Sorry. You never know anything in California." For no apparent reason, he began telling us about climbing out on his hotel balcony with a few buddies, then swinging from flagpoles until the police removed him. "Everyone else got away, but what can you—SHIT!" Ray from Ontario did a backflip, right there on the streets of Venice, California. "Goddamn! That was Bob Hope! In that black limousine there. Did you see that black limousine?"

Bob Wakefield and I craned our necks to see, several blocks away now, a black limousine.

"Are you sure Bob Hope was in there?" Bob said.

"Swear to God. I swear to God it was Bob Hope. I saw his nose. He waved."

"You played hockey," I ventured. "Didn't you?"

"Fourteen years. Well, gents, gotta run. Somewhere in this town, there's a party with my name on it."

V enice City Beach was covered with far more cigarette butts than beachtowels; we walked several city blocks in the sand before it became obvious that we were never going to find our spot. So we traipsed back to El Basurero and drove to Santa Monica State Beach.

"This is probably a good idea," Bob said. "I felt nervous parking there. I saw someone peek through a curtain. I mean, we could've been towed. I didn't budget any money for that."

For a moment I considered telling him about Grandpa Bob's last insurance hundred, zipped into the side compartment of my shaving kit and bouncing around in the trunk. This would provide a welcome respite from his financial worries, but I honored my grandmother's pledge to secrecy.

We found our spot: a clean, vacant sandy patch adjoining two redheads, one of whom lay on her stomach with her top off. Five hours later I woke up and went off to write postcards and listen to the car radio. Bob lay sprawled in the sand, looking very much like a corpse. Back on the benchseat of El Basurero, I was pleased to be responsible for getting it here, beachside, providing the seventeen-and-a-half-year-old machine with such a pretty view in its twilight years.

When Bob finally awoke, he placed the first of several phone calls to Larry's apartment. There was no answer.

"He *does* know we're coming, right?"

Bob waved me off. "I wrote him before we left. And I mailed him a postcard from Estes. He knows. He probably just isn't home from work yet."

It was six o'clock.

I wrote postcards to everyone I was supposed to: eight of them, including a two-parter to Laura. I wrote gibberish, stream-of-consciousness stuff to old roommates. I wrote a funny one to my sister. I told Mimi that we'd neither broken the bank nor lost our shirts in Vegas but thanks again for the bankroll. In extremely small handwriting, I summarized the last four days for Laura, four days being the amount of time since I'd last called or written. But writing to her made me miss her, and when I finished writing, I mailed all the cards and immediately headed for the nearest phonebooth to call Columbus collect.

"I feel like going on a date," I said, and that did sound wonderful: being bathed and freshly shaven, my immediate future promising dinner, a good new movie and dozens of doors to hold open. Instead, I told her, I stood in the California dusk, waiting for a stranger to return from work so I might sit down in a chair.

"I hope you're getting everything from this trip that you wanted to get out of it. Don't get mad, but I'm starting to miss you."

"I'm not mad." I couldn't have loved her more.

Before we finished talking, I learned that the bridesmaids' dresses were complete.

For another hour I watched scores of skateboarders and rollerskaters shoot down the sidewalk, perfect specimens of beach-culture enthusiasts.

Bob finally reached Larry, and on our way over, at a BP station, a Dodgeful of black teenagers admired El Basurero without sarcasm and even offered to buy it, which left me aghast but Bob blasé. "I could probably sell it and pay for plane fare home. Cars like this are a big deal out here." He swelled, visibly, with pride. "You can't find cars like this one anymore."

The second thing that made it quite clear that we were in a galaxy far, far away was Larry's mammoth apartment compound. Spraddled across a hillside in Culver City, the place could've housed each of Bryan, Ohio's, 8,000 residents. Larry met us in the lobby, then led us through a mind-numbing series of stairways, courtyards, pool decks, mezzanines, hallways, corridors, elevators—a circuitous route he insisted was the fastest way. We would stay there for five days, and each time we entered or exited, I considered leaving a trail of breadcrumbs to assist the search parties.

Larry drove a large American car not unlike El Basurero, except that it was five years younger, a different color and free of peculiarities in the exhaust system, the upholstery and the suspension. But it, too, was a big ugly thing that originally was owned and driven by parents, and had journeyed here from Ohio. So when Larry offered us an autotour of the Sunset Strip and other storied places, neither Bob nor I felt terribly displaced.

We passed the Whiskey-A-Go-Go, Mann's Chinese Theater and the restaurant where owner Alan Hale—the erstwhile Skipper of "Gilligan's Island"—now spends his time, and I couldn't tell you about any of it. Sleep dogged me through these places I'd always wanted to see, dogged me so effectively that I all but gave up, content to let the neon and tinsel and squalor blur, content to close my eyes and smile at Larry's endless string of jokes about illegal-alien kitchen help and their lack of Green Cards, content to be so far away from home.

We jerked to a stop at the Griffith Park observatory, in the Hollywood Hills, overlooking the Greater Los Angeles Basin. Shaken awake to walk around, I didn't find the dreamlike expanse of starlight and streetlight as daunting as I might have.

"I don't know what's gotten into this town," Larry said, laughing. "Really, I don't. Did you know this is the official observatory of the 1984 Olympics?" He bent over and snatched up a handful of Griffith Park turf. "And here we have the official blade of grass of the 1984 Olympics." He surveyed the basin. "Imagine tourists from all over the world driving down there, tourists who can't read English. It'll be gridlock." He stopped at a little vending machine, which, for 75 cents, would forge a six-inch facsimile of the Incredible Hulk from molten plastic. "You drove in here today. Can *you* imagine the Olympics in L.A.?"

"We don't know," I said. "We're tourists, too."

"Your Hulk's done," Bob pointed out.

By the end of his shift, the joke must seem stale to the Phantom of the Opera. But we tourists love it—his act makes the wait for the Universal Glamour Tram a pleasure.

"That's a real guy," I whispered to Bob. "You see that statue of the Phantom of the Opera? That's a real guy."

Bob raised an eyebrow, then nodded. *Oh yeah.*

The only reason I knew this wasn't a statue was that, ten years before, one of his predecessors—a wolf-man, I believe—caused my mother's heart to lurch.

The Phantom displayed patience, waiting until the line had progressed far enough that no bystanders had seen him move. Then he grasped the shoulders of a nearby nun, who screamed and clutched her hands to her chest. But then she smiled, a smile not of for-giveness but of thanks, a smile that complemented the joke.

The line filed toward a batch of empty trams, and the Phantom resumed his pose. We had played statues on my grade-school playground, but none of us were as good as this Phantom. Universal Studios had applied money and technical expertise to co-opt childhood amusement, which is nothing new in Holly-wood.

Behind us a man shouted and laughter floated from the tourists around him.

On this late June after-noon, our tram pulled up a cavern chiseled into a snowy hillock, which, our tour guide assured us, had been used in "The Six Million Dollar Man."

"I remember that one!" Bob exclaimed.

Once inside, our tram was menaced by robots as a synthesized voice whirred something about exter-minating the Earthlings. Then entered a white-coveralled blond actor wielding a laser—no prop this—and began incinerating evil Cylons.

Rather than run, we sat, and the tram carried us safely into the daylight. Eyes met—eyes of husbands and wives, of parents and children, of friends and friends—in a communal gloat of accomplishment.

"Dave!" Over the intercom our guide feigned horror. "Dave, you're not going to drive over that old bridge! It won't *hold* us, Dave. You and your short-cuts!"

Had we encountered this bridge on some blue highway in El Basurero, I would've felt the same way. But not in Hollywood. My fellow tram-mates and I beamed as Dave steered us onto the old bridge, rushing to focus our Nikons as timbers dropped off and pilings disintegrated, assured by a tiny voice in our subconscious: "it's only a movie, it's only a movie."

Surprise: the tram reached the other side at the precise moment that the bridge fell into the ravine.

When we rounded a bend and could see the bridge's steel superstructure, the tram paused to let us watch the bridge rebuild itself. We'd been hood-winked, of course, but we all *wanted* to fall for it, which is why any reservations about this obvious stunt were drowned out by applause.

Tourists receive just enough technical information at the special-effects soundstage to become boorish at any movie they later see that contains a special effect.

Robert Wagner starred in the little movie we saw about "the power of illusion," and sounded not unlike Scott Free. There were pauses in the dialogue for him to "interact" with the tour guide, who had to remember to interject the scripted repartee at just the right moment. Wagner narrated special-effects clips, the greatest hits from the films of the Lumiere brothers up to the films of Lucas and Spielberg. Interspersed with the film were real-life demonstrations, some of which featured lucky members of our studio audience.

We saw a ferris wheel from Steven Spielberg's bomb *1941* roll off a pier, and from this we learned the impact of table-top effects.

We saw two young lovers outfitted in space garb in a cutaway cockpit of a starfighter. The screen behind them ran a film loop of an asteroid shower, and from this we learned the principle of the matte.

We saw a small boy on a bicycle—with E.T. swaddled in a blanket and tucked into the handlebar basket—ride across the moon, pedaling with great vigor, waving to his parents, and watching himself on the studio monitor, and from this we learned the difference between mere special effects and a well-made icon.

Back on the Glamour Tram (a registered trademark of Universal Studios, Inc.), we chugged through the backlots, cameras drawn and blazing. Our guide told us which facades had graced which films as we broached abrupt transitions from the Old West to New York City to European Village to Norman Bates's house to Suburbia to Sleepy Mexican Town. When informed that a tame, pink, bay-windowed split-level had been the film home of "Leave It to Beaver," "Marcus Welby, M.D.," and (in *Bedtime for Bonzo*) Ronald Reagan, we gasped on cue and photographed a house that looked like most of our next-door neighbors'.

Much had changed since my last visit. One new addition was the large *Jaws* exhibit—the Amity Island set coupled with an appearance by Bruce the Mechanical Shark. This had become the highlight of the tour, to judge from the disappointed moans when it was announced that Bruce was undergoing repair and would be scaring the shit out of none of us.

The parting of the Red Sea no longer thrills a single tourist. With memory of Cecil B. DeMille dim, the attraction is now the Red Sea's contents: a half-submerged police car with, cemented to its roof, a statue of George Peppard in a dragon suit. This was merely the first of our encounters with "The A-Team." Statues of the cast members were scattered about, and children were provided with scorecards to record their sightings. There was even an A-Team Action Show, a 3,000-seat arena where stunt doubles of A-Team cast detonate marauding hippies and Mexicans.

Years before, the only attractions in the Entertainment Center were the Stunt Show and the Animal Actors' Stage, each of which were (and still are) about what you'd expect: stuntmen bouncing off tin roofs; hawks, cats, monkeys and dogs behaving as if they understood English.

Now it's a full-blown amusement park. Were one to take only the tram tour, Universal could be done in a morning. But getting around to the five live shows eats up a day. Bob and I, of course, got our money's worth, sitting down near KITT the Talking Car (from the TV show "Knight Rider") to coordinate show times. Pretty precise stuff, too, allowing for visits to the eleven giftshops and the Woody Woodpecker Museum in between waits for the A-Team show and "Conan: A Sword and Sorcery Spectacular."

Our final stop, at 7:55 P.M., was the Screen Test

Comedy Theatre, where Bob and I succeeded in being chosen from the audience to star in an honest-to-God movie, one of six essentially identical videotapes produced every day. Still, a movie with us in it. Hot damn. Our hands shot up without hesitation. I was cast as a desperado, Bob as a feisty ten-year-old named Buster. "The desperadoes get wet," the emcee warned. "They have to jump in that tank. Just so you know."

With my fellow hombres, I was whisked backstage for costuming. "You know," I told the production assistant, "I swam in college."

"Wow, this could be the start of something big," she said. "Just like Johnny Weissmuller, right?"

I realized what a jerk I must have sounded like. "Right."

They even provided brand-new underwear, in addition to which I wore a floppy black hat, a vest, a white shirt, and huge butternut chaps made of compressed life jackets.

The plot of our opus involved the misadventures of a sack of cash, which the desperadoes acquire by holding up an Old West bank—where cute lil' Bob/Buster played a terrified onlooker. Next we find ourselves on the edge of a cliff and—in desperation, and after executing a you-go-first slapstick routine—must leap into the water below. The cash bag flies free, and passes through the hands of (to name only a few) barn-storming pilots, picnicking Gay Nineties lovers and the Blues Brothers, who crash through the wall of the Old West bank, where the money returns to its rightful depositors, who celebrate with an epic pie fight.

We tourists were quite the actors, flubbing cues, laughing on camera, leaping into the water tank on top of the heads of our brothers-in-crime. At the film's world premiere—held about twenty minutes later—the audience seemed delighted by the spliced-in scenes from old B-movies, and by us. Us! Many who had watched the rehearsal sat through the final cut, and some of them weren't even related to a cast member. At the end of the film, when Bob/Buster swaggered up and splattered the bad guys with a shaving-cream pie, they laughed louder than audiences at many a real movie.

The Screen Test Comedy Theatre subsidizes its new underwear by selling thirty-dollar videotapes of the performances. I suppose the whole thing's a bit cynical, but I did consider breaking Grandpa Bob's insurance hundred to buy one, even when I remembered I didn't own a VCR. But God, how fun to jump into a vat of water on a hot summer day, dressed in silly clothing, and then to drip dry as I watched my best friend, dressed even sillier, apply a pie tin to the face of a stranger.

On the way out, I realized this was the first day we had not received our daily Elvis. Before I had a chance to feel sad, I had to laugh at my literal-mindedness, because of *course* we had.

The next morning, at a red light somewhere in Anaheim, a Monte Carlo with New York plates pulled alongside us. The driver, an Arab, rolled down the window and gestured with the urgency of a man whose wife was giving birth. "Deezneylahnd!" he shouted. We stared as he employed both hands and an even wilder look in his eyes. "Deezneylahnd!"

We didn't know just where it was. I'd gone the wrong way when we'd left the Santa Ana Freeway because I wanted a doughnut. Then road construction had prevented us from retracing our steps, so we began circling through Anaheim, figuring that a glimpse of a spire from Cinderella's castle would guide us.

"Christ," I told Bob, "I don't know what to tell him."

"Wait, there it is. Look back there. It's the Matterhorn."

"Deeeezneylahnd!" the man demanded.

I pointed to the white bump on the horizon.

He spotted it, nodded his thanks, threw back his head in laughter and—tires screaming—ran the light.

When my parents still owned Winegardner Mobile Homes, they attended two industry RV shows each year: one in South Bend, the other in Louisville. Even the phrase "the Louisville show" sounded romantic to me. I had no idea what went on there—and my imagination conjured up showgirls and champagne, not Airstream brochures, paunchy sales reps and Porta-Potti demonstrations. Still, because I never went to one, the shows remained romantic.

That notion became even further separated from reality when, one year, my parents returned from the South Bend show and announced they had won, as a sales award, a trip to Spain. I ran upstairs to look at Spain on my globe. A week later I learned that it was a trip for *two* to Spain, and for the first time in my life, to my great and abiding despair, my parents took a week's vacation without me.

The following year, Mom and Dad returned from the Louisville show with the news they had won yet another trip, this time to Honolulu. Once burned, I knew better than to rush to the globe. Besides, I knew where Hawaii was. Sure enough, Shari and I stayed with Mimi and Grandpa Bob in south central Illinois while Mom and Dad went to Hawaii—where I was *sure* there were showgirls and champagne. What a waste.

Once the oil embargo hit, sales awards became a memory and I gave up any hope that Mom and Dad might ever win that elusive trip for four. So a few years later, when I was twelve, I was suspicious of their announcement that—as a doorprize from the Monsanto booth—they'd won a family pass, including admission to the Monsanto V.I.P. lounge, to . . . Disneyland.

There was a catch. We had to provide our own way from Bryan, Ohio, to Anaheim, California. But try telling two children that you've won free V.I.P. admission to Disneyland but haven't quite decided whether the family can afford the transportation.

We spent two weeks that summer just getting to Disneyland, my parents improvising stops in hellhole history museums over Shari's and my strenuous objections. After that kind of build-up, I began to fear that Disneyland might be disappointing. Since we'd taken a family vacation to Disney World a few years back, the theme-park experience wasn't exactly novel. And the Monsanto V.I.P. lounge (where I expected, naturally, showgirls and champagne) was an Astroturfed conference room in which we were treated to a soggy box lunch.

But Disney World isn't the patriarch of theme parks all the world over. It doesn't have a Matterhorn and it wouldn't matter even if it did, because Disneyland simply isn't going to play the role of a disappointment in anyone's past. They have that all worked out.

On our way out, bleary from a long, happy day and too many ice cream novelties, I convinced Dad to buy me a 36″ × 48″ map of Disneyland. Back home in Ohio, the first thing I did was tape it to my wall, where it stayed for the next eleven years, until my parents sold the house.

Bob and I paid $2 to park, whereupon the attendant handed us a ticket stub and a green folder entitled "The Best Ways to See Disneyland," which included a map of the parking lot and the admonition: "DON'T MISPLACE YOUR CAR. Indicate on the parking map your approximate location . . . then keep this folder with you." Bob scrawled an *X* in Lot H.

The folder also explained the different admission policies. When I'd been here before, Disneyland still employed the loathsome ticket booklets, requiring excursions on stupid half-assed rides because you had B-Tickets to burn and forbidding a second ride on the Matterhorn because, alas, the E-Tickets were long gone. All over the park, parents and children used to huddle in packs, debating the most judicious use of the remaining tickets.

Disneyland has changed from ticket booklets to Passports, which provide Unlimited Use of the Attractions. The Passports may be purchased for one, two or three days, at prices of $14, $24 or $31. In addition, there is a three-hour guided tour for $5, although I can't imagine what sort of dunderhead would require such a service. After all, this is a place with thirteen clearly marked "picture spots," from which any comptroller from Kalamazoo can snap photos identical to those on the giftshop postcards. This is a place that supplies everyone with a free four-color, 24-page brochure containing, among other things, an overall map, detailed maps of each of the seven park sections, listings of every restaurant, snackbar and giftshop, and two full pages of photography advice. On top of *this,* they offer a guided tour?

In the abstract, I suppose it's sinister that Disneyland has removed free will, that in their desire to keep the blacktop cleaner than most of their guests' bathtubs they have created idiot-proof fun. But the hell with anyone who really believes that. The most wonderful thing about Disneyland is that you can simply give yourself over to it. The most important decision Bob and I had to make all day was whether to proceed through the park clockwise or counterclockwise.

Characteristically, we strove to get our money's worth by riding every damn thing at least once. Our first ride—according to our map, Attraction #1 in Tomorrowland—was "Adventure thru Inner Space," based loosely on the film *Fantastic Voyage* and consisting of a pod on a conveyor that circles through a building where screens and lights and tubes simulate the world of the molecule, then of the cell. We sped through the far reaches of the universe in Space Mountain, then strapped ourselves into a sweaty, half-submerged submarine for a slightly undersea voyage with Captain Nemo. We even ventured onto the Autotopia, actually enduring a line for the privilege of driving little cars with lawnmower engines, a ride that's not particularly thrilling for anyone with a driver's license. But we rode this one and, when we happened across a similar ride in Fantasyland, that one too.

Fantasyland, in fact, proved a momentous sector. First and foremost we thrice rode the Matterhorn—the zippiest rollercoaster ever tucked into an ersatz Alp—hurtling through impossibly small caverns and around suicide switchbacks, feeling relief from the June sun not only from the breeze but also from mounds upon mounds of designer snow, convincing enough to create a comforting, psychosomatic chill.

Then next took our places in a gaily painted dinghy that floated us through the interminable, insufferably saccharine "It's a Small World." I harbored hatred for this ride ever since my parents decided to squander *four* E-Tickets so that we might be subjected to endless renditions of that damn song (seven in every known language) lip-synched from the mouths of billions of satanically cute dolls, all the while slumped in the hard seat of the mankind's slowest-moving water vessel. But in 1984, on the Passport system, it seemed safe to return, if only to see if childhood's anger could be transmogrofied into an adult indulgence of the transcendentally bad. I still found the ride quite a bore, but I figured a good use for it. "You know, the first place Khrushchev wanted to go when he first came to America was Disneyland."

"Yeah," Bob said. "I'd heard that."

"What we have to do is figure a way to get Reagan and Chernenko in here. Then we tie them to one of these boats and they'll have to ride it over and over until they come up with a solution that will guarantee world peace forever." We sailed past a thousand hula-ing dolls. "It'll either work or they'll do the honorable thing and commit seppuku."

"It's worth a shot," Bob agreed, wincing at Masai figurines forthcoming. "Personally, I could live with the seppuku. No pun intended."

"None taken."

Finally, Fantasyland's topper: the Mad Hatter's Tea Party. Unsuspecting tourists board teacups, only to find that their cups whirl one direction, their saucers another, the sickening stripes on the floor of the ride still another—all of which conspires to cause stomachs full of soda pop and greasy doughnuts to implode. This ride was the first thing Bob and I had talked about, five years before in freshman English. As vague nausea set in, we took pictures of each other to commemorate the event and cement history. Staggering to a grassy knoll to recover, we bumped into a middle-aged couple. They were holding hands and wearing identical Elvis Presley T-shirts. Rather than excusing myself, I mumbled my thanks and grinned at Bob. We shook hands.

"You know, this is the longest day of the year," Bob said. "The summer solstice."

Nearby, a crew of Disney employees inserted poles into the blacktop and strung ropes between them, readying the area for a parade of ducks, the second of the day. Donald Duck would turn fifty in 1984, and Disneyland was celebrating this milestone several times a day for the entire year—with precisely the same parade.

"How American." Bob surveyed Fantasyland, striving for perspective. I couldn't tell if he said that with awe or contempt.

We could hear the first strains of Donald's birthday anthem, which sounded enough like Stevie Wonder's Martin Luther King tribute ("Happy Birthday") to conjure visions of the world's oddest lawsuit.

The sun stayed immobile in the sky as we methodically tripped through Frontierland, Bear Country, New Orleans Square and Adventureland, edging inexorably toward Main Street, U.S.A. We rode a

riverboat and runaway train, survived 999 appa-
ritions in a haunted mansion, hung out with boozy
Pirates of the Caribbean. We climbed through a tree-
house that any child would prefer to his own home.
"But all this," I kept telling Bob, "is nothing compared
to the Enchanted Tiki Room."

Anthropomorphism lurked around every
gilded corner; animated bears and moose performed
in a musical review, jungle shores teemed with remarkable mechanical facsimiles of frolicsome
giraffes, zebra and hippopotami. Dozens of costumed
cartoon characters redefined ubiquity. But even this,
I reminded Bob, "was nothing compared to the Tiki
Room."

One hundred tourists sat in a tropical hut, waiting for the show to begin. Soon, above our heads, it
did: four talking parrots descended on their perches,
representing—with cliched accents—England, Ger-
many, France and Mexico. They exchanged silly ban-
ter and we supplied the laughter.

Each MC/parrot sang. Several female cock-
atoos joined in, and Pierre L'Parrot cajoled one hundred human beings into song: "Let's all sing like the
birdies do," we bellowed, no voice holding back.
"Cheep. Cheep cheep. Cheep cheep."

Gargantuan beds of flowers glided down from
the ceiling, and they, too, sang: daffodils handling so-
prano and alto, snapdragons and dahlias assuming
tenor and bass.

The MC/parrots precipitated the mayhem of
the finale, abetted forthwith by the full complement of
tropical birds. The flowers joined in, upping the cho-
rus to something like seventy-five voices. Then, along
each of the four walls, dozens of decorative stone idols
sprang to life, beating on their primitive tom-toms as
frenetic Polynesian percussive effects tested the woof-
ers of the room's speaker system. On the room's eight
support beams and its four doors, the totem carvings

opened their eyes and mouths and burst into song. A rhythmic, castanet-like clicking was supplied by the afflicted blinking of the eyes in the walls and doors. In joy and fear, wonder and bemusement, every tourist reached down deep to hit the high notes:

In the Tiki, Tiki, Tiki, Tiki Room,
In the Tiki, Tiki, Tiki, Tiki Room,
Oh, the birds sing words and the
      flowers blo-o-o-o-o-o-o-om,
In
The
Tiki, Tiki, Tiki, Tiki Room.

The strangest thing of all: we shuffled out after the show ended, smiling and generally behaving as if we'd just experienced nothing more miraculous than a situation comedy.

Bob discovered a video trivia game in an arcade along Main Street U.S.A. He'd never seen one like it before, but on the first play he racked up the machine's fourth-highest score, whereupon he raced to the cashier for five bucks' worth of quarters. Outside I picked my way through the day's final duck parade, which was waddling noisily down the street. There was a phonebooth catty-cornered to Town Hall, just beside the free kennel. "I'm so glad you called!" Laura said. "Where are you?"

"Disneyland."

"Good news! Guess what—we have an apartment. Isn't that great?"

It *was* great. Laura and I had been looking for a place we could afford since May, and though we'd placed our names on waiting lists galore, we'd heard nothing. I'd avoided thinking about what might happen if we never heard; in fact, I had buried the issue so deep that it took me a moment to identify the wobbly feeling in my legs as the passing of anxiety. In only a month we'd be living in our first apartment. We would be married. At times I'd worried that this might not be such a good idea, but that evening—2,270 miles from Laura, with a monorail whooshing by—I could imagine nothing that held more promise. We laughed together; everything in creation seemed resolved and ambiguity slid from every issue.

"C'mon, Bob. Let's go."

Embroiled in the bonus questions, he didn't respond. I waited for him to finish. The machine's top nine scores belonged to one "RJW."

"C'mon, Robert John Wakefield. I'm beat."

We stopped for ice cream, then dawdled down Main Street, U.S.A. toward the parking lot.

"Hey," Bob said. "We didn't see that." The building he pointed to, according to our guidebook, contained an assortment of Disney awards and memorabilia, as well as an "Audio-Animatronics tribute" to Abraham Lincoln.

"I'm beat."

"Fine," he said, still studying the place. "I wonder why they chose Abraham Lincoln?"

"You mean, as opposed to Walt Disney?"

"Yeah." Bob tossed his ice cream cup into a shimmering trashcan. "Or as opposed to, say, Elvis."

I mulled that over. "Okay, but then they'd have to change the name of Main Street, U.S.A., to Elvis Presley Boulevard."

14

If I Get Home
on Christmas Day

W e were planning to go
to San Francisco next. The restoration of the street-
cars had just been completed, and this seemed like
something we ought to see. For two days, though, we
lay sprawled across Larry's floor, lethargic and blank.

On Friday we got up at nine and spent the day
paging through the *Los Angeles Times*, discussing
what we might do. There were any number of bands
to see, drives to take, wax museums and amusement
parks to sample: too much for a kid who'd grown up
in a place where the main streets shut down during
July to make way for a carnival called the Bryan Jubi-
lee. On a legal pad I listed everything that sounded
promising. I filled two pages, but we left the apartment only once that afternoon—to purchase sandwiches and, for Laura, a pair of shorts sporting the
official logo of the 1984 Olympics—and once that
night—to go bar-hopping in Westwood with Larry.

Though he'd lived in L.A. for more than a year,
he seemed to know less about the local hotspots than
we did, the result of which was an evening spent in a
series of undistinguished hotel bars, some of which

(oh, kiss of death!) revolved. The entertainment consisted primarily of doing tricks with matches in the
ashtray, and our drink orders were no less embarrassing: mostly sorority-girl stuff, frozen and sweet. To
compensate, I downed a clutch of martinis and rumi-
nated about focus.

After last-call, we passed three young men,
armed with leaflets, from Jews for Jesus. "Coming
soon: the sequel to end all sequels!" one shouted. "It's
not *Rocky XII*. It's not *Superman IX*. It's not even
Another Returning Jedi."

"Halleluia!" cried another. "It's guaranteed to
break all box office records. It's guaranteed to break
all box offices."

"Do you know what it is?" the third yelled at us.
We all avoided making eye contact.

In unison, the three answered their own question. "It's *The Return of Jesus!*"

"Oh," Bob said, taking the offered pamphlet as
a souvenir without breaking stride, "will there be ma-
tinees?"

Amidst the laughter of bystanders, an answer
was no doubt offered. But by then we were homeward
bound.

On Saturday we decided
not to go to San Francisco or anywhere else except
back to Ohio. Bob cited poverty and fatigue, as I did
(although, with the insurance hundred in my shaving
kit, the former was a lie). Having decided to leave at
night, when the desert might be kinder to El Basurero,
we killed the day with Larry, riding into the mountains in his car to research the setting for a chase scene
in a screenplay he was writing. I enjoyed the drive up,

if only because it was a pleasure to climb a tortuous mountain road without hearing clacking valves and other disturbing automotive ailments. The road, I was certain, had already been used in countless movie chase scenes. Still, we were treated to a spectacular view of the Los Angeles basin, spread out before us like a mammoth train set, intricate and smokey. The view almost justified the three hours we spent waiting in a doughnut shop for the Shell station's on-duty mechanic to get to Larry's car, after—on the way down the mountain—the brakes caught fire and three fledgling Buckeye writers barely escaped with their lives.

I assumed, from family-vacation experience, that once we'd made the decision to turn around, the trip was over and all that remained was 2,231 miles of blindered anticlimax. Tourism had officially been sacrificed at the altar of making good time. So I climbed into the backseat and slept while Bob drove the first leg. Near Sunday's dawn, we made our first pitstop, in Las Vegas.

I screamed.

"Relax," Bob said, parking in a sidestreet off the Strip. "Do you want one of their industrial cheap-o breakfasts or don't you?"

I relented, but I held my breath as we walked past the slot machines. After we sucked up our prefab $1.57 eggs-bacon-and-homefries and dozens of ancillary cups of joe, Bob dumped 50 cents into a slot machine. "I'm driving," I insisted.

"Why?"

"Insanity. You're insane. You couldn't afford San Francisco and here you are chucking quarters."

He shrugged. "Could have won. And, besides, it's not illegal to drive in Nevada if you're insane. This state is a pioneer in that twisted field of the law."

"We'll be in Utah soon," I said. "And you know what that means."

Bob handed me the keys.

On the way out of town, we passed a billboard advertising the appearance of an Elvis impersonator in the Legends in Concert show, and it didn't need to be said. "There must be lights, burnin' brighter," I sang instead. "Somewhere,"

Bob joined me: "Got to be birds, flyin' higher, in a sky, more bluuuuuue."

We followed I-70 from its very headwaters, somewhere in darkest Utah, where its status as an American interstate highway is more bravado than pavement. Radio stations disappeared into the endless buttes and thrust-faults of Fishlake National Forest and Big Rock Candy Mountain, but we let the static play, a tide of white noise preferable to silence or to our eighteen spent cassette tapes.

Just past the Colorado border, I-70 began to flank the Colorado River, which it would do for 200-odd miles. And odd miles they were, too, since the river was swollen from melting mountain snows and in several places had caused a lane or two of interstate to tumble into the drink. We drove past countless sandbags, flagmen and restraining walls, climbing and climbing and climbing, until we reached Vail Pass, where, in the highest roadside rest area on Earth, El Basurero refused to move.

We'd come back from the rest room and it flat wouldn't make noise. The car had given us some tense moments before, but it had always spoken to us, gasps and hisses that said *Wait, boys, just give me some room, some air, some time to catch my breath*. Bob turned the key. Nothing. After he let it cool down for a few minutes, he tried again. Nothing. And a few minutes later, still nothing.

"Do you know what it is?" I had put off asking this, hoping there would be no need.

Bob wouldn't answer.

"Is there, um. . . . Can I do something? How about some water?"

He bowed his head to the wheel, then ran his hands repeatedly through his hair. He started making a noise, one so soft that I had to wait for it to gradually increase in volume for me to recognize it as a groan.

"Should I pop the hood," I asked.

Again, the hair thing. Finally he sat back in his seat. "Did you see a phone up there?"

"No."

"Well, go look." He tried the ignition, and again El Basurero made no sound. "I think it's dead."

"You want me to call an undertaker?" I'd meant this as a joke, but it was a mistake and too close to the truth. Bob glanced at me as if I were leprous, then got out to perform the autopsy. Failing to find a telephone, I climbed up into a mountain meadow, yelled a few profanities and sat for hours with my head between my knees, occasionally getting up to watch Bob minister to our ride home. Home! Had I found a phone, I would've called Laura before any towtruck.

Near evening, Bob found the loose ignition wire and El Basurero chugged to life. I sprinted down the mountain, afraid I'd be left. We didn't speak much, all the way to Estes Park.

We were in Estes for a week, waiting for Joan to get official word from the owners of the Black Canyon Lodge that—even if pummeled by wolverines—they absolutely, positively forbade the employment of another waiter. Eventually this happened.

We waited for a call from a roommate of a friend of Bob's who lived in Colorado Springs and sought cheap transportation to Valparaiso, Indiana. This would've cut our expenses, so we tried to contact him. But apparently he was enjoying a string of one-night stands, since his roommate kept telling us that he hadn't come home the night before but was certain to show up at any minute. I waited for Bob to lose patience, and eventually this happened.

I also waited for Bob to decide whether he wanted to stay in Estes Park, job or no job. The Wakefields were having a family reunion there at the end of July, and Bob couldn't see much point in leaving only to drive all the way back.

And I waited for the courage to tell Bob how desperate I was to leave. It was time to go home. I called Laura and told her how much I wanted to be with her, how this waiting felt like the world's most protracted layover for a connecting flight. Because Bob's family continued to be gracious hosts and proficient cooks, I couldn't bring myself to tell him how that week-long high-altitude stasis had begun to eat through my stomach lining.

Most of all, we waited for the energy to get back on the road. Eventually this, too, happened.

Leaving Estes Park, we decided to make the Denver-to-Oxford interstate corridor in a time that we could brag about. So we planned our fuel stops well in advance, dividing responsibilities and racing around in Midwestern service stations as if pursued by the Feds. Even when the muffler fell off in western Kansas, we stopped for only five minutes, scarcely long enough to secure, with coat hangers, these miscellaneous chunks of metal to El Basurero's rusted underbelly. Bob did this as I waved traffic around us.

In central Missouri, long after dark, Bob searched the radio dial for a newscast. "I wonder if we've missed anything in the world? The world probably won't let us back in."

"Did that ever happen," I asked, readjusting my pillow for the hundredth time since Topeka. "Did you ever come home from vacation and find out something big had happened the week before?"

He stroked his unshaven chin and retied the T-shirt he was using for a bandana. "Nixon, when I was in Colorado one summer. On television they were talking about 'President Ford' and we were saying, 'Who's he'?" Bob gave up and switched off the radio. "You?"

When the memory came back, I shook myself awake. "God. I just thought of this. Elvis."

Bob looked at me, eyebrows arched in skepticism.

"No, really," I said. "It was on our last family vacation. I read about it in a Portland, Oregon, newspaper." I hadn't thought of this even once since it had happened. "They used color photos of the funeral, which I guess was the day before."

"That's no daily Elvis," Bob said. "That doesn't count. I'm *sorry.*" He began steering the car with his knees. "That's Elvis of Christmas Past."

I took out our tattered, filthy map, paging to the Transcontinental Mileage Chart, which said that St. Louis lay only 283 miles from—I suddenly realized—

where we had to end this trip. "It's not that far. I mean, it's far, but not ridiculous."

"What's not?"

"Memphis."

Bob stared eastward as the numbers on mileage signs to St. Louis shrank to double digits.

"Well?" I said. "What have we got to lose? You wanted that Elvis ashtray, remember? Let's go get it."

"We're low on gas. I think we can make it to St. Louis. Maybe we can."

"Hey, maybe it's Elvis International Tribute week now. I forget when that was, but maybe it's now. It could be." Excited, I began to bounce in my seat. "God, of course it would be. We could go see Elvoids from all over the world. I mean, imagine the van-murals!"

Bob rubbed his eyes and steered with his elbows.

"What do you think? Is this perfect or what?"

He groaned. "Or what."

"C'mon. What vacation is complete without an Elvis ashtray? We missed *all* the souvenir shops. All of them. If memory serves, there were two blocks of buildings devoted to the Elvis industry. Two blocks!"

"No."

"Think about it," I said. "I mean, didn't you learn *anything* from the Miracle Photo? Didn't that tell you something? Hey, maybe we could nose around and find out what's upstairs."

"No." Bob studied the gas gauge, moving his lips as he made calculations.

"If it's money—" I began. *Don't just spend this,* Mimi had said. *That's just for emergencies.* "I have a little left. Enough to cover us."

I tried to lure him into discussing this, but Bob kept silent until, on the outskirts of St. Louis, he delineated our responsibilities during the impending fuel-up.

"You pump," he said. "I'll squeegee the windows and pay. Then you drive."

"Sure, fine."

"And we're not going to Memphis. We're going home. You're getting married and I believe it's the responsibility of the best man to see you get there, that you don't wind up in the Memphis hoosegow for desecrating the sacred bathroom." He looked over to gauge my response. "I'm right. It couldn't be anything but a letdown."

Now it was my turn to sit in silence as I-70 slid underneath me and Ohio beckoned. When I considered the 280 miles to Memphis, the 280 miles back, the who-knows-how-many days we'd spend doing it, I knew with absolute peace that I didn't want to go back to Graceland. Though any quest seeks not the end of the road but the road itself, any American quest seeks not whimsical resolution but the dedication to a new and more challenging quest. Doubling back just won't do in the land of manifest destiny.

"You're right," I said.

"Yeah." Bob smiled—just barely, but he did smile. "What are friends for?"

"Thanks for doing this," I said. "The trip. Other stuff."

"We're not home yet," he said, pulling into an Amoco. "Every mile El Basurero achieves is a challenge and a surprise."

We laughed, then attended to his car like Olympic bobsledders just before a run, got the seventeen-and-a-half-year-old hulk back on the road and then hunkered down for our final leg. In our rearview mirror I could see the ostentatious Gateway Arch—lit up at this late hour by banks of halogen lights. Up ahead, if I looked hard enough, I could see an inevitably disappointing apartment building and the love of a good and patient woman.

Epilogue
Can't Help
Falling in Love

Bob Wakefield forgot his pants. He'd hurried back to Ohio from his new home in Virginia, and forgot to bring a pair of gray pants. So as the first guests arrive at the church, Bob and I race through the men's department of a store in the Eastland Mall. He'll settle for the first decent pair that fits, as there's no time for aesthetics or alterations.

Brad Coleman and Tom Richissin, a boyhood friend and a college friend, hook up their microphones and strap on their guitars. They survey the gathering audience until a cue is given for them to start their six-song medley, which begins with the sole Elvis Presley song, "Love Me Tender," then proceeds through Sam Cooke, John Lennon and other primo rock 'n' roll balladeers, finishing with a song written for the occasion: music by Tom and Brad, words by Tom and Brad and Bob Wakefield. The set wasn't recorded and the song is lost. David Gretick, who watches from about six pews back, later says it was terrific. Margy Janus Coleman, although she admits her bias, will concur.

My college roommates and spring-break travel companions usher in the guests.

In a back room of the church, Shari arrives only a little bit late. The directions were not perfect, and my sister still has some problems with geography. She apologizes, but Mom tells her not to fret, that her brother the groom arrived only minutes before. Then Mom goes to the narthex and straightens Dad's tie. They embrace. This is August, vacation month. One of the few Augusts in the past twenty-five years they will spend entirely in Ohio.

In the sacristy, I amass five wedges in my first three turns. I lack only the orange, Sports and Leisure, my best category. Bob has the blue Geography but nothing else. Pastor Risch, who is about to perform my wedding ceremony, looks on, impressed. But on the threshold of Bob's first loss ever in the Genus Edition of Trivial Pursuit, I quit, too nervous to roll the dice. Bob obediently packs up the game. "That's all right," he says. "You would've won. I concede."

"That's very gracious of you," I say.

Pastor Risch claps each of us on the shoulder, smiles, adjusts his robes and goes out to check last-minute details.

She is beautiful. She is beautiful, not in the soulless bride-magazine way, with an overwhelming white dress and plastic hair.

Laura is beautiful because she is Laura, because she has chosen a simple dress and omitted the stupid, elaborate veil. I take her right hand from her father's arm, and we advance to the altar. It's all I can do not to laugh. I'm having too much fun to be afraid.

The seats of Laura's new Mazda recline. The finish is still perfect. Our friends have filled its ashtrays with rice and stuffed the interior full of balloons. On the back window is a sign: "He got her today, but *she'll* get *him* tonight." Our friends and relatives—nearly a dozen of whom I've traveled with—stand at the door of the restaurant with their hands in their pockets or on their hips. They're about to go home, but my wife and I are now, officially, on vacation.

In the morning Laura and I clean up the car and light out for Myrtle Beach—I-70 east, I-77 south, I-20 east. I have booked a room in an expensive hotel at the opposite end of the strip from the amusement park and Ripley's Museum and (as I've been told) yet another talking Jeannie. The room is more than I can afford, but I have the security of knowing where I can lay my hands on a quick $100.

In western North Carolina, no more than three hours from Gatlinburg, an Elvis Presley song comes on the car radio.

"Give us this day our daily Elvis," I mutter. "I mean, *my*. No, *our*. Our daily Elvis."

Laura looks up from the book she is reading. "What?"

We cross the South Carolina line. "Oh, nothing," I say, a little embarrassed. I switch stations, and stop when I hit something classical. I have no idea what I am listening to, but I like it.

Vita

Mark David Winegard-
ner was born in 1961 in Wauseon, Ohio, because
his parents didn't like the hospital in Bryan, Ohio,
where they lived. He is an American citizen, a
registered voter and an all-around good guy. He graduated from Bryan High School, in 1979, worked in
a brass mill in the summer of 1982 and, that same
year, received a speeding ticket on his twentieth
birthday. He received his Bachelor of Arts in English from Miami University, Oxford, Ohio, in
1983, graduating magna cum laude and Phi Beta
Kappa, and was employed as a bartender from
June 1983 to April 1984. He has won a number
of fellowships and writing contests that nobody
really cares about, and has published fiction in "little magazines" as well as *Playgirl*. He has, in the
past two years, gradually renewed and then expand-
ed his childhood love of baseball, and now believes
that the sun rises and sets on the Cincinnati Reds.
He is currently employed by the City of Fairfax,
where he writes newsletters, directs the cable-cast-
ing of city council meetings and drinks a danger-

ous amount of coffee. His favorite beer is Guinness, but he most often drinks the far cheaper Schmidt's Light. He lives with his wife, Laura, in Fairfax, Virginia.